WHEN SIX-GUNS RULED

WHEN SIX-GUNS RULED

Outlaw Tales of the Southwest

by
Marc Simmons

Ancient City Press
Santa Fe, New Mexico

International Standard Book Number:
0-941270-64-5 clothbound
0-941279-63-7 paperback

Library of Congress Catalog Number:
89-082081

First Edition

Cover Art by Glen Strock
Book design by Mary Powell

For Linda and Trinidad Padilla

CONTENTS

SOUTHWEST

PREFACE

Outlaws of the Old West is a subject that holds a perennial interest for many people. The desperados and gunfighters who blasted their way into the pages of history were bloodthirsty rascals at best. But many of them led colorful and dramatic lives, so that their stories—more than one hundred years later—provide plenty of entertaining reading.

For a long time popular fiction, Hollywood films, and television dramas have drawn upon the personalities and themes of western banditry to attract an audience and in so doing have met with considerable success. Sure to be a crowd pleaser is any presentation that features the likes of Jesse James, Billy the Kid, the Daltons, Belle Star, Johnny Ringo, or Black Bart. Lives of most of the better-known outlaws are clouded in myth, but part of their attraction seems to be in the opportunities afforded for dissolving legend and bringing to light, at long last, the truth.

This book deals with a couple of dozen outlaws, and even a few lawmen, who made some sort of splash on the southwestern frontier during the nineteenth and early twentieth centuries. The names of several, like William F. Bonney, alias Billy the Kid, and Clay Allison, will already be familiar to readers of regional literature. But most of the others are virtual unknowns whose stories have been buried and, until now, forgotten. Men who went by such curious titles as Coal Oil Johnnie, Russian Bill,

Kid Barton, and Black Jack Ketchum got sideways of the law, and before matters worked themselves out they frequently ended up dangling from a rope or suffering a fatal case of lead poisoning. That was usually enough to propel their names into the frontier newspapers, now preserved in archives, and then, of course, court records tell more of their personal histories, or anyway, the end of their histories.

As this little volume of outlaw sketches is intended for the general reader, it contains no academic footnotes and no comprehensive bibliography. Nevertheless, a list of "Suggested Readings" has been attached at the end to aid those who might wish to delve deeper into the fascinating and often complex saga of frontier lawlessness. The references given naturally reflect the preferences and prejudices of the author.

For help along the way and for general encouragement I would like to thank Evelyn Vinogradov, Archie West, Liz Dear, Lawrence Clark Powell, Mark Gardner, John Kessell, Susie Henderson, and Lois Hughes. As on previous books, my gratitude also extends to Mary Powell of the Ancient City Press.

Marc Simmons
Cerrillos, New Mexico
May 15, 1989

New Mexico, in the heart of the American Southwest, experienced an unusual amount of disorder and crime during its formative period. In their best-selling book, *Violence in America*, authors Hugh Davis Graham and Ted Robert Gurr say that the territory was the only place in the nation where assassination became an integral part of the political system, from the end of the Civil War down to about 1900.

Just why this was the case, they are hard pressed to explain. But they do suggest that violence in New Mexico, characterized by brutal Indian wars, vigilante movements and lynch mobs, feuds, land grant wars, and outlaw activities, created such an unwholesome climate that it skewed the political system in the direction of assassination as a useful and effective tactic to eliminate troublesome opponents. The authors conclude that explanation of "the frightening phenomenon of assassination in territorial New Mexico still awaits searching study by the historian."

Governor Miguel A. Otero (1897-1906) once offered his own observation to account for the prevalence of lawlessness in his native land. "New Mexico," he wrote in his memoirs, "was located so as to receive the backwash from two streams." One stream flowed from the east (Texas and the Indian Territory), while the other flowed from the west (Arizona and California). These two dark and sinister currents spewed out their human refuse, claimed the governor, so that New Mexico became a catch basin for rogues and desperadoes from elsewhere. There is much in the historical record that would seem to confirm Otero's opinion.

Because New Mexico Territory remained undeveloped so long, possessed plenty of empty canyons and mountain wilderness where men on the run could lose themselves, and lacked strong agencies of law enforcement (nothing like the famed Texas Rangers or Arizona Rangers), it became an outlaw haven. That situation, however, prompted a vigorous response from honest citizens who sometimes took it upon themselves to maintain order and public morality. When justice seemed too slow or the few sheriffs too weak, they formed secret committees of vigilantes.

Although they never gained the national notoriety of similar groups in frontier California and Montana, bands of New Mexico vigilantes nevertheless played a significant role in freeing their communities from the sort of badmen Governor Otero complained about. Vigilante cells were especially active in Albuquerque, Las Vegas, and Socorro, but it was the last of these communities that witnessed the worst ill effects that could spring from citizen-justice.

Socorro in the 1880s was a wide-open mining and cattle town. A dozen saloons and gambling halls catered to *pistoleros* from El Paso, rustlers from the high plains, and hardrock miners from the Magdalena Mountains to the west. The local sheriff found it impossible to keep the violence in check, so Socorro folk formed a Safety Committee to dispense justice on their own. This body was also known popularly as *Los Colgadores*, The Hangers, owing to the frequency and speed with which it prescribed the rope.

The vigilante group in Socorro, which had started out to uphold the law, let power go to its head and ended up committing as many abuses as the outlaws. It forced citizens to join the organization against their wills, and it strung up several innocent persons. As a result, public pressure in 1883 forced the Safety Committee to disband. But before that happened, the vigilantes staged one last spectacular hanging, that of Joe Fowler, described later in this book.

When one recalls the many shootings and lynchings associated with New Mexico's territorial era, it is tempting to infer that murder and mayhem have always been part of life in this corner of the Southwest. But not so! During the three hundred years of the Spanish colonial period, major crimes of any sort were comparatively rare. The judicial records, still preserved at Santa Fe, admittedly are incomplete, but enough remains to confirm that homicide was practically unheard of.

One notable exception was the murder in 1806 of a wandering French fur trader named Jacques D'Eglise. Two men arrested for the crime were Antonio Carbajal and Mariano Benavides, residents of the town of La Canada north of Santa Fe. The *alcalde*, or magistrate, of that place conducted the court proceedings, the documents from which unhappily have been lost.

What we know of the affair comes from a letter of Governor Joaquin Real Alencaster sent to the royal high court of Guadalajara. In it he says, "In the trial records the crime is found so fully proven and it

3

is so horrible that it will be most useful in this province of New Mexico if the punishment be prompt and exemplary. This will necessarily impress the minds of other citizens who are unaccustomed to seeing the infliction of capital punishment."

The Guadalajara court agreed and ordered the executions. The sentence was carried out by the *alcalde* of La Canada. In his official report, the governor stated that the guilty parties were shot and then, in his words, "I had their bodies hung out on the Camino Real for the length of time which seemed to be fitting to make an example of them."

Few today would condone hanging the bodies of murderers on the interstate highway. But the treatment accorded the killers of Frenchman Jacques D'Eglise does seem to have had some salutary effect. At least, we can find no further instances of homicide in what remained of the colonial years.

Even during the territorial period, beginning in 1850 and extending to the achievement of statehood in 1912, New Mexico had a large lawful element among its population, although the numerous and much-publicized shoot-outs, hold-ups, and political assassinations tended to suggest otherwise. All across this remote frontier, a high premium was placed on honesty, and every man was considered to be responsible for his own actions.

Ranch houses, line camps, and even homes in mining boom towns were customarily left unlocked. Everyone took it for granted that nothing would be disturbed. Also, the code of the day allowed hungry travelers to enter ranches or line shacks when the owners were away, prepare a meal, and eat their fill. But they were required to wash up their dirty dishes afterward.

At the wild and woolly camp of Shakespeare, New Mexico, near Lordsburg, one resident kept $30,000 in a baking powder can on a shelf in his house. The money sat there for years, known to everyone in the community, and it was never touched. At White Oaks, a mining center on the other side of the territory, merchant W. H. Weed for many years sold liquor in a unique fashion. In a side room, off his main store, he had a barrel each of rye and bourbon with a handy supply of jigger glasses. Customers entered the room alone, served themselves, and as they left through the store, they made a signal to the clerk, indicating the number of drinks consumed. The clerk entered the amount in an account book, accepting without question the individual's word.

And there was the case of the desk manager who worked for a hotel in a small town in Torrance County, east of Albuquerque. That was soon after the turn of the century when the old New Mexico Central Railway served the area. The manager was accustomed to retire early, closing the front desk by eight o'clock. Trouble was, a late train arrived after that hour, usually bringing a salesman, cattle buyer, or some such to the hotel. A sign at the desk told them to deposit money in the unlocked register, take a key from the wall, and find their own room. Often the guest was up and gone before the manager came down next morning. But in twenty years at the job, he would say after retirement, no one had ever rifled the cash register, nor had anyone failed to deposit his room rent.

Incidents such as these—and many others could be furnished by way of illustration—lend weight to the view that there were plenty of upright

5

and law-abiding residents on the southwestern frontier to serve as a counterbalance to the hordes of outlaws. Unfortunately perhaps, it was the lawbreakers who grabbed the headlines and whose names continue to loom large in the history books. Part of our continuing fascination with the Wild West derives from the colorful and violent careers of members of the outlaw fraternity. But surely another part, too, comes from learning that the vast majority of old-time evildoers met untimely and often violent ends, seeming to prove that justice will win out.

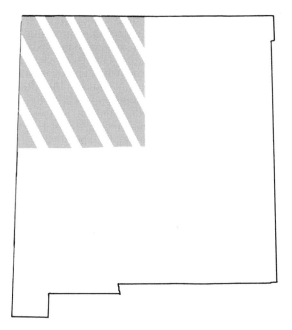

War in San Juan County

In the early days, lawlessness in San Juan County, New Mexico, gave the Four Corners region a hard and unsavory reputation. The worst period of violence occurred during 1879 and 1880. Outlaw gangs rode the countryside unchecked, and lynchings were said to be as common as fleas on a dog.

Unlike the much-publicized conflicts in Colfax and Lincoln counties, this "war" has received little attention. The reason probably is that very little of it makes any sense.

Newspapers of the day report a long string of bloody incidents, but it is seldom clear who was upholding the law and who was breaking it. Desperados sometimes wore badges and vigilantes occasionally engaged in criminal acts.

At the center of the conflict were the Stocktons and the Coes. While their roles are not always clear, at least their personal histories offer us a visible thread to follow.

Ike and Port Stockton were raised on a ranch near Cleburne, Texas, south of Dallas. Both were hot tempered. Port is said to have killed the first of a dozen men when he was only twelve years old.

In their late teens the brothers went to Colfax County, New Mexico, and became involved in the land grant war. When Port murdered a man in Cimarron, Ike broke him out of jail and they fled.

After a couple of more killings, Port went to Animas City in the southwestern corner of Colorado. Fast talking got him the job of town marshal.

But one day when he was getting a shave, the nervous barber nicked him with the razor. Port whipped out his pistol and shot the barber. Arrested, he escaped and crossed the line into San Juan County.

Meanwhile, brother Ike had gone to Lincoln and opened a saloon. He became friends with the Coe family, particularly the cousins Frank and George, who were allied with the McSween faction in the local war.

After the Coe ranch house was burned to the ground, several of the family decided it would be healthier elsewhere. They moved to the Farmington area.

Ike Stockton went too and stopped briefly at Port's new ranch in San Juan County. Then he moved across the state border to Durango.

Soon Port was using his ranch as a base for cattle rustling. Other rustlers were operating in the district, and as a result ranchers formed a Stockmen's Protective Association. As policy, they hanged all suspicious characters who fell into their hands.

Some accounts claim that Ike had his own gang of rustlers, but that is not certain. He paid frequent visits to Farmington to visit his brother and Frank and George Coe.

One day a posse from the Stockmen's Association followed a trail of stolen cattle that led to Port Stockton's ranch. He came to the door with a rifle and was riddled with bullets. Mrs. Stockton grabbed

General Lew Wallace, Governor of New Mexico, 1878-81, in his study at Crawfordville, Indiana. Courtesy Museum of New Mexico. Neg. No. 40340.

a gun and went after her husband's assailants. In the shoot-out, she was wounded but later recovered.

It is said that the death of Port touched off the San Juan County War. Enraged, Ike Stockton vowed to track down and kill the members of the Association posse who had slain his brother. One of those was Frank Coe.

Ike, with a band of outlaws he collected, did manage to gun down several of the men on his list.

His reign of terror brought out armed citizens to patrol the dusty streets of Farmington.

Governor Lew Wallace in Santa Fe posted a reward of $2,250 for the capture of Ike Stockton and his gang. He also appointed the San Juan Guards, a local militia unit, to serve as a police force.

But the violence continued until one frosty day in late October, 1881. Ike brazenly rode into Durango for supplies and was quickly confronted by the sheriff and his deputy.

In an exchange of shots, a bullet shattered the outlaw's knee. He was carried to a doctor's office where his left leg had to be amputated. Within a few hours Ike Stockton died, from loss of blood and the shock of the operation. So ended an unsavory career.

With the passing of their leader, members of the Stockton gang, numbering more than one hundred, broke into small bands and went their separate ways. One group staged some hold-ups in northern New Mexico, then fled to the Black Range west of the Rio Grande.

Later they appeared in Socorro where they were recognized and arrested. That same night a party of vigilantes seized the outlaws and hanged them from a tree on a side street. Afterward, the street was known as "Death's Alley."

In the early 1880s, the Coes returned to Lincoln County where things had quieted down. In 1931, George Coe wrote his autobiography, published by the University of New Mexico Press under the title *Frontier Fighter.* In it he related his many scrapes in the Lincoln and San Juan county wars. George Coe died in Roswell in 1941.

The Provencher Murder

Apparently no historian or other writer has ever pulled together the story of the murder of Captain Dumas Provencher in 1888. It happened at the little village of San Rafael, a few miles southwest of present Grants.

The crime earned banner headlines in newspapers of the day and sent shock waves all the way to the territorial legislature. So it seems strange that the case should have been left out of the history books. Here's what is known about the matter.

Sometime before 1874 Dumas Provencher came to the New Mexico Territory, evidently for the purpose of homesteading. He settled at San Rafael and there met and married Maria Brun.

Maria's brother was the local priest, Father Jean B. Brun, who was a French Canadian. He had built a large European-style house in which he conducted Mass for several years until a small frame chapel could be constructed nearby.

Although nothing is known of Provencher's background, it is probably a safe guess that he, too, was a French Canadian—his name would suggest that—and likely he knew the Bruns earlier in Canada. Indeed, they may have persuaded him to come to New Mexico when Father Brun assumed his duties here as a parish priest.

Dumas Provencher and his wife apparently moved around a bit in western New Mexico. It is recorded that he established and operated a sawmill in a village called La Jarita. Later he moved to Blue-

Dumas Provencher, ca. 1879-84. Photo by W. Henry Brown.
Courtesy Museum of New Mexico. Neg. No. 10343.

water where he was involved in buying mules for the government.

By the early 1880s the Provenchers were back in San Rafael. Two of their young children died in these years, possibly in an epidemic, and were buried inside the little chapel built by Father Brun.

In time Dumas became a captain in the First Cavalry Regiment of the New Mexico Volunteer Militia. His commander was Lieutenant Colonel Walter G. Marmon, a teacher and trader at Laguna Pueblo who had married into the tribe and become governor over the Indians in 1886.

The men in Dumas's company were Hispanics from San Rafael and vicinity, who were his friends and neighbors. They called him Don Damacio.

In the summer of 1885 Apaches were on their last warpath in central New Mexico, and the militia was called out to scour the lava beds south of Grants. Captain Provencher led several scouting parties in pursuit of the hostiles, but no Apaches were found and it was the last Indian campaign in which the unit participated.

This, in sum, is about all that is known concerning Dumas Provencher and his career in New Mexico—other than a few details surrounding the circumstances of his untimely death.

It was election time, November 1888, and Dumas and his brother-in-law, Father Brun, were designated as poll watchers in San Rafael. Two Indians came into the hall and were denied ballots by Captain Provencher. Indians at that date had not been granted citizenship and so could not vote.

That evening after the poll had closed, the Captain was watching the tallying of the ballots. Suddenly a shot rang through the window and he slumped to the floor, dead.

It was said that another election official shot out the lamp and plunged the room into darkness. When the lights went on again, Provencher's death was confirmed.

From the beginning the crime was regarded as a political killing. The family of the victim offered a large reward, and Territorial Governor Edmund G. Ross asked the legislature to offer an additional reward for information on the slayers. However, the governor's attempt to conduct an investigation was sidetracked by partisan forces in the legislature who seem to have been bent on protecting the guilty parties. Walter Marmon, a friend and former commander of Provencher's, declared with disgust that "personal likes and dislikes, partisan hate and ignorance rule the actions of legislative members."

Ross was an unpopular reform governor. Provencher had supported him, and according to conventional wisdom, he had paid for that support with his life. No evidence was ever produced and the murder remained unsolved.

In the aftermath of the tragedy, Father Brun also had his life threatened. One rumor held that he had to flee San Rafael in the dead of night, disguised as a woman! He afterward took the parish at Socorro on the Rio Grande and died there in 1907.

Following the shooting, Dumas Provencher had been buried in the little frame chapel of San Rafael. That building continued as a local landmark until it was destroyed by a fire in May of 1930. The townspeople to this day are convinced that Don Damacio was the victim of an organized conspiracy that had its origins in Santa Fe.

Violence in Politics

During the 1890s Santa Fe was rocked by what one historian has described as "the most deplorable series of murders, assassinations and tragedies ever registered in the chronicles of the capital." At the center of the storm were Francisco (Frank) Borrego and his brother Antonio.

The trouble started after the city elections of 1890. Frank Borrego, a Democrat serving as coroner, had a squabble with the County Commission, which replaced him with another Democrat, Jose Gallegos. Borrego was so angry that he turned Republican, taking many of his friends and relatives with him.

Later, Borrego chanced to meet Gallegos at a dance hall on San Francisco Street. Hot words passed between the two men, and they adjourned outside to settle their differences with a fight. Things got out of hand, spectators joined in the ensuing brawl, and Frank Borrego pulled a gun and shot his rival in the head.

He was at once marched off to jail. There he was chained to a post buried in the ground and soon afterward received a severe beating from the jailer, Juan Dominguez, a friend of the slain Gallegos.

Poor Borrego complained to Sheriff Francisco Chavez about his treatment. The sheriff replied that he had gotten just what he deserved, and to drive the point home he administered a pistol-whipping about the head. As a result of this second drubbing, Frank Borrego was temporarily blinded.

At the trial, Borrego luckily had Thomas B.

Catron defending him. Catron was head of the Republican political machine and one of the richest and most powerful men in the territory. On a plea of self-defense, he managed to get his client off for the killing of Jose Gallegos.

Now free, Frank Borrego went to Colorado to recuperate and recover his eyesight. Before departing, he swore vengeance against the men who had beaten him in jail. By May of 1892, he was back in Santa Fe.

On the 29th of that month, Francisco Chavez, who had recently left office as sheriff, was walking home after dark. Crossing the railroad bridge over the Santa Fe River at Guadalupe Church, he was felled by a hail of bullets. Neighbors running into the street failed to catch a glimpse of the assailants.

When jailer Juan Dominguez learned of the death of his former boss, he was gripped by panic. However, instead of fleeing he decided to go looking for Borrego. "Santa Fe is not big enough for the both of us," he told friends. But his ambush from a hiding place near the cathedral backfired. His first shots missed, and Frank Borrego gunned him down with a Colt .45.

For this latest killing, Borrego again got off with self-defense. His attorney Catron, who himself had narrowly escaped an assassination attempt a short time before, proved that he was adroit in keeping fellow Republicans out of jail.

But times were rough and politics dirty. Some unscrupulous Democrats saw a chance to damage Catron's reputation by pursuing, if not actually railroading, his friend and client, Frank Borrego.

Time drifted by and at last Frank was indicted

The bridge over the Santa Fe River by Guadalupe Church, Santa Fe, New Mexico, site of Francisco Chavez's murder on May 29, 1892, and shown here with the last narrow gauge freight crossing it. Photo by Margaret McKittrick. Courtesy Museum of New Mexico. Neg. No. 41833.

for the murder of former Sheriff Chavez. His brother Antonio, and two companions, named Alarid and Valencia, were also named in the indictment.

The thirty-seven-day trial created a sensation around the territory. On May 29, 1895, exactly three years after the slaying of Chavez, the four accused were found guilty and sentenced to hang. An appeal was made at once to the Territorial Supreme Court. The evidence had been circumstantial, the defendants maintaining their innocence and claiming they had been in a card game at the time of the murder.

Also, the conduct of the trial had been surrounded by numerous irregularities. During the proceedings, Sheriff William Cunningham, a Democrat, was reported to have played poker with the jurors, given them cigars, and even taken them out to a nearby racetrack to see his horse run.

Nevertheless, the Supreme Court upheld the verdict. Over the next several years, the condemned men received no less than six stays of execution, two of them coming upon appeals to Presidents Cleveland and McKinley to commute the sentences.

Time finally ran out on April 2, 1897. The condemned were marched to the scaffold amid tight security. Friends had threatened to rescue them at the last moment. But the executions were carried out, although it was not certain at the time that justice had been done.

To this day, some historians contend that the Borregos and their friends were victims of a political conspiracy. The full truth of the affair may never be known. But the case serves as a good example of the dark and violent character of political life in territorial New Mexico.

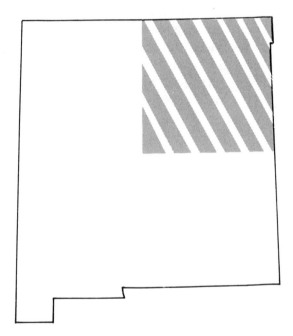

NEW MEXICO

Trail Robbers

The old Santa Fe Trail began in the Missouri border towns, stretched across the Kansas prairies and into southeastern Colorado, crossed the heights of Raton Pass, and came to its end at last on Santa Fe's historic plaza. Opened in 1821, the trail in its nearly sixty years of history was witness to some of the most stirring events in the saga of the great West.

While not common, incidents of outlawry did occur at times on the Santa Fe Trail, but most of them have been forgotten or at least overlooked by writers of western history. One of the earliest episodes occurred in 1864, according to a published report in the *Santa Fe Gazette*.

It seems one of New Mexico's prominent merchants, Don Antonio Manuel Otero, had dispatched east a large freight caravan under his *mayordomo*, or wagonmaster. As the train approached the summit of Raton Pass, it was held up by a party of bandits professing to be Texans.

The *mayordomo* was carrying a large sum of money to make purchases for Don Antonio in Kansas City. This was stolen, as well as all the saddle and draft animals, whose loss left the caravan stranded.

"The story of the robbers being Texans is discredited," editorialized the *Gazette*. "They are supposed to be men who knew the value of the train and who put on the guise of Texans to escape detection and punishment."

General Henry Carleton, military commander of New Mexico, sent out soldiers to pursue and arrest the guilty parties. But nothing has come to light that would suggest they met with any success.

The significance of the crime is suggested by a statement in the *Gazette*: "This is the first robbery of the kind that has ever been committed on the road between New Mexico and the States."

Some years later, a stagecoach of the Barlow and Sanderson Company was held up in Raton Pass with bloody results. The express messenger and two passengers were shot and killed and about $60,000 taken. The culprits, identified as Kit Barton and his gang, made their escape.

A large posse went in pursuit and finally caught up with the offenders near the future site of Tucumcari. A fatal shoot-out followed in which the Kid gunned down a sheriff and two deputies. But those were his last killings. He was captured and summarily hanged from a convenient bridge.

Kid Barton seems to have been overlooked by even the best-informed outlaw buffs. So too has been a non-descript road agent who generally went by the handle, "Coal Oil Johnnie."

By the laws of nature, Coal Oil must have had parents, and doubtless they gave him a respectable last name at birth. But what that name was, no one seems to remember today.

About 1872, according to New Mexico's territorial press, Coal Oil Johnnie teamed up with another misfit named Tom Taylor, and the pair went

The stagecoach held up by Kid Barton and his gang in
Raton Pass. Shown here in the patio of the Palace of the
Governors, Santa Fe, New Mexico. Photo by Betty Theil.
Courtesy Museum of New Mexico. Neg. No. 11950.

to holding up stages along the Santa Fe Trail.

Said the papers, "They scared everybody badly with their daring stagecoach robberies," and, "They were pretty tough to have rattled the ribs of such old stage drivers as Uncle Billy Hubble, Charley Evans, Jim Aney, and Jim Abercrombie."

Nor was that all. One contemporary account spells out the grim details. "It was the custom of Johnnie and Tom to stop everyone, and often in coming up to a traveler on the lonely road they would ride alongside of him for a time in the most peaceful manner, talking cheerfully and seeming in the best of humor.

"Then, one of them would turn suddenly to the stranger and say: 'I am tired of your company,' and in the next instant the poor traveler was shot dead and left on the prairie to feed the coyotes."

The Barlow and Sanderson Company, operator of the main stage line on the Santa Fe Trail, lost so many strongboxes that it offered a large reward in a bid to stop the exploits of the two bandits.

The famous Maxwell Land Grant Company, then owned by some wealthy English capitalists, also got into the act by posting rewards of $2,000 each for the heads of Johnnie and Tom. As one newspaper headline advised readers, "The war was on to the finish."

Reports claim that as word of the rewards circulated two demure gentlemen from Texas, Jim McIntyre and Frank Stewart, put on their war bonnets and headed for New Mexico. They were bounty hunters.

Striking the Santa Fe Trail, they rode up to Collier's Soap Factory, seven miles from Fort Union at the foot of the Turkey Mountains. There they hid in the lava rocks and set an ambush.

Shortly, the two outlaws came by on their way to the robbing of another stage. But that was as far as they got. A hail of bullets brought them to the ground and ended their misguided careers.

"The victims were shot full of holes and their miserable remains were taken to Cimarron," declared the news story of the incident. "Somebody at Henry Lambert's hotel took a door off its hinges and to this the dead bodies were tied. When the door was stood on end, the bodies were photographed. Taylor was an exceptionally tall man while Coal Oil was the proverbial short one."

The Texas bounty hunters collected their $4,000 for the ambush at the soap factory. It is said that they remained in the territory for several years, eventually becoming outlaws themselves. McIntyre later returned to Texas where he was slain by the celebrated gunfighter Luke Short. Stewart also fled New Mexico, and he is not heard of again.

Incidentally, Lambert's hotel in Cimarron is today called the St. James. It recently re-opened and is in the process of being restored. Bullet holes can still be seen in the ceiling of the room that was once a saloon.

The Outlaw and the Nun

In 1872 a twenty-two-year-old nun received orders from her mother house in Ohio to go west and begin missionary work in Trinidad, Colorado. Sister Blandina Segale traveled by train and stagecoach to her new station in a strange and violent land.

Trinidad sat at the northern entrance of Raton Pass, the gateway to New Mexico on the Santa Fe Trail. When Sister Blandina stepped off the stage, she could scarcely believe she was still within the United States. Spanish was the language heard in the dusty streets, for the small sprinkling of Anglos had not yet managed to "Americanize" the town. And most men carried guns strapped to their legs, for here the six-gun still ruled.

For four years the good Sister taught and nursed, winning the hearts of the local people. Then in 1876 came orders from her superiors to move on to new fields in Santa Fe and Albuquerque, places where she was destined to leave a small but lasting mark on history.

It was in Trinidad, though, that she experienced one of the most curious episodes of her entire career in the Southwest. It brought her into a strange relationship with a young outlaw and to a meeting with Billy the Kid and his gang.

The matter began with a couple of young fellows, known to be associates of the notorious Kid. The pair had got to drinking in Cimarron, New Mexico, and ended by shooting up the place. They fled to Raton Pass and on the Colorado-New Mexico line fell to quarreling. The disagreement ended in a shoot-out. One was killed and the other, a six-foot-three lad named Phil Schneider, received a bullet in his leg. The wounded man was found by travelers and carried to Trinidad where he was rudely tossed into an abandoned adobe hut.

Several days later Sister Blandina heard about

Sister Blandina Segale, S.C. (1850-1941). Courtesy Museum of New Mexico. Neg. No. 67735.

the matter. "The general sentiment around town," she related, "was, 'Let the desperado die.' " But she was quite unwilling to do that.

Gathering up food and water, soap and linens, she went to the hut and stepped inside. The ferocious-looking outlaw was lying in the corner, and the Sister was terrified. Fear caused her to blurt out, "I see that nothing but a bullet through your brain will finish you!

"I saw a quivering smile pass over his face, and his tiger eyes gleamed. My words seemed heartless. I had gone to make up for the inhuman treatment given by others, and instead, I had added to the inhumanity by my words."

"Well, Sister," the man replied, "I'm very glad you came to see me. Will you come again?"

Sister Blandina readily agreed and thus began daily visits that extended over a long period of weeks. One day the patient told her, "That first day you came, if you had spoken to me of religion and repentance, I would have ordered you out. But when you said that about the bullet in the brain, you have no idea what strength and courage those words put into me!"

And then he asked, "Sister, do you think God can forgive me?" And, when assured that all was possible, he said that he would relate some of his awful crimes.

For long he had been in the habit of murdering and robbing travelers on the Santa Fe Trail. He would look for persons who had missed the way and send them off on a false trail. Then he would follow, kill them in their sleep, and take their valuables.

Another time he had been stealing cattle in Kansas. An old rancher and his cowboys had caught him and promptly prepared to hang him from a cottonwood. Young Schneider had begged for his life, so the men relented. Later when he rejoined his companions, the outlaw spoke of the incident and the other men laughed.

Angry, Schneider declared he would go find the old rancher and bring back his scalp for a bet of ten cents. A week later he returned with the bloody scalp and collected his wager.

Sister Blandina listened in stoic silence to all his tales of horror, then heard the young man conclude, "Through you I believe God is leading me to ask pardon for my many devilish acts."

One morning the desperado announced that Billy the Kid was coming with some of his friends, not only to pay a visit but to scalp the four doctors living in Trinidad because they had failed to remove the bullet from Schneider's leg.

Sister arranged to be present at the hour of their arrival. Said she: "The leader, Billy, has steel-blue eyes, peach complexion, is young, one would take him to be seventeen—innocent-looking, save for the corners of his eyes, which tell a set purpose, good or bad. The others are all fine looking young men."

Billy expressed his gratitude for the care she had given Schneider and offered to extend her any favor. That was the opening Sister Blandina was looking for.

"Yes, there is one favor you can grant me."

"Whatever it may be, it is yours," answered Billy.

"I understand," Sister continued, "that you have come to scalp our Trinidad physicians, which act I ask you to cancel."

A deathly silence suddenly filled the hut, but at last Billy replied, "I granted the favor before I knew what it was, and it stands." So, Sister Blandina, by using her wits, had saved the doctors and averted a tragedy.

A few weeks later, Schneider took a turn for the worse. As the end drew near, Sister knelt by his side and whispered some final prayers. And he told her good-bye.

"That was the end of my services to the tiger desperado," Sister Blandina wrote sorrowfully in her diary. "I left him to the mercy of God."

The Gentleman Outlaw

It was said of badman Clay Allison that he never picked a fight and never avoided one. He was a curious desperado, loved by some and hated by many more. In that, perhaps, he resembled his contemporary, Billy the Kid.

Had Allison died like the Kid, at a young age in a blaze of gunfire, he would be better remembered today. But he lived well beyond his gunslinging years and met his end alone in an accident along a country road.

The manner of his death was perhaps predictable because by some unlucky alignment of stars he was born accident prone. His birthplace was Tennessee, 1840. Soon after he entered this world, little

Clay suffered a serious head injury that seems to have left him with a permanent mental disorder.

When the Civil War broke out, he joined the Confederate army. But within months he was discharged for emotional instability. At war's end, he drifted into Texas and won his spurs as a cowhand working for the famous cattleman Charles Goodnight.

From the Texas period comes the first of a legion of hair-raising stories that one day would form the Clay Allison legend. It is said that he got into a dispute over a water hole with a man named Johnson. The two agreed to fight to the death in novel fashion.

First they dug a grave, each politely taking turns because there was only one shovel. Then both men leaped into the deep pit and went at one another with Bowie knives. The fray was furious and bloody. At its conclusion Clay alone emerged, but with an ugly wound in the thigh. Crippled as he was, he managed to push enough dirt into the hole to provide his foe a decent burial.

The wound left one of Clay's legs shorter than the other, so that he limped the rest of his life and rode horseback with one short stirrup.

That, of course, cannot properly be rated as an accident. But fate, awaiting the appropriate moment, had another in store for him. Later in his career, Clay Allison accidentally shot himself in the foot. One of the few surviving photos of the man, taken shortly after the mishap, shows him seated with his foot bandaged and crutches at his side.

About 1870 Allison left Texas and took up ranching near Cimarron in Colfax County, New

Mexico. It was here that he earned his reputation as a gunfighter. In his first shoot-out, he killed an outlaw named Chuck Colbert at the Clifton House, a stage stop on the Santa Fe Trail.

But what brought him to prominence was his participation in the Colfax County War that burst upon the territory in 1875. The conflict had its origins in a series of problems over the huge Maxwell land grant and the corrupt dealings of the notorious Santa Fe Ring.

Although Allison had little use for the law and believed in settling matters with his own six-gun, he was also possessed of a strong sense of fair play. Therefore, in the war he sided with homesteaders (even though he was a rancher) who were opposed to the ring.

In the summer of 1875 the Reverend F. J. Tolby was assassinated, it was believed on order of the Ring because he had criticized its illegal dealings in a national news story. Allison led a lynch mob that strung up the alleged murderer on a telegraph pole. When a Ring man, Pancho Griego, confronted him in the local saloon, Allison left him dead on the floor.

Other shootings followed and a reign of terror descended upon Cimarron. One night a drunk Allison took out his anger on the town newspaper by throwing the press into the river and blowing up the office.

The following morning, much sobered, he returned to view the ruin. Unexpectedly he found a pregnant Mrs. Ada Morley, wife of one of the newspaper's owners, standing in front of the burned out office crying.

St. James Hotel, Cimarron, New Mexico, ca 1920. Clay Allison was a rancher and gunfighter in the Cimarron area during the 1875 Colfax County War. Courtesy Museum of New Mexico. Neg. No. 49157.

When she saw Allison, she gave him a severe tongue lashing. At the end of the tirade, he pulled out a roll of bills and thrust them into the lady's hand. "I don't fight women," he announced. "Here, go buy yourself another press."

The following year, Clay Allison killed a deputy sheriff in Colorado. Somehow he escaped a murder conviction. Next he turned up in Dodge City. There, he was reported to have gone on a shooting spree, forcing Bat Masterson and other lawmen to run for cover.

Later Clay married a respectable woman and went back to ranching in Texas. But he did not entirely abandon his unpredictable ways. Once he rode horseback through town stark naked. On another occasion he went to a dentist and the man pulled the wrong tooth. So he threw the dentist into a chair and pulled one of *his* teeth.

And the freak accident that killed him? He was returning home in a wagon from a drinking bout. A sudden chuckhole threw him to the ground and the rear wheel ran over his neck.

Neighbors laid him to rest in a grave beside the Pecos River. Under his name on the tombstone were placed the words: "He never killed a man who didn't need killing." On the frontier that was a handsome tribute.

Justice by the Rope

As Americans we appear to be a people of extremes. If today justice is lax, the opposite often held true a hundred years ago. Then it was stern and unforgiving, whether by court or by vigilantes. A case in point occurred at Las Vegas in the days when New Mexico was still wild.

It began on a cold January night in 1880. A gang of four horse thieves was in town, heavily armed, and was visiting the saloons in rotation. By their last stop the quartet was thoroughly drunk and getting mean.

City Marshal Joe Carson braced them alone in the Close & Patterson Saloon with orders to surrender their pistols. The men refused and abused him with offensive language. Within moments a brisk gunfight erupted. Before it was over, at least forty shots had been fired.

The marshal was hit nine times. All the outlaws were wounded, but two of them, Tom Henry and John Dorsey, escaped to the livery stable, climbed on their horses, and fled north.

Marshal Carson crawled through the dance hall on his hands and knees in hopes of reaching home and seeing his wife before the end. But as he met her at the door, he fell forward face-down, dead.

One of the remaining outlaws soon died and was buried that same night without ceremony in a pauper's lot. The other, James West, was dragged off to a jail cell still bleeding.

The incident created the greatest excitement in Las Vegas and surrounding San Miguel County. A week passed and then it was learned that Henry and Dorsey were hiding out at a friend's ranch near the town of Mora. A posse formed on the Las Vegas plaza and set out at once, determined to bring them back dead or alive.

At Mora the fugitives' hideout was surrounded. Henry and Dorsey gave up, but only after exacting a promise of protection from mob violence and a fair trial. Riding back to Las Vegas a captive, Tom Henry decided he had made a mistake in surrendering.

He attempted to bargain with the posse. "Allow me a hundred yards head start," he pleaded, "and then you can fire after me with your rifles. I'll take a chance of getting away." The deputies refused his offer but renewed their promise of protection.

In the Las Vegas jail the three surviving bandits were interviewed by newspaper reporters. Tom

Henry, the twenty-one-year-old gang leader, declared that while he and his companions had come to town to steal horses and have a good time, they hadn't planned on killing anyone. It was all a bad mix-up, caused by drinking too much whiskey, he said. James West, age twenty-two, told the reporters that Henry and Dorsey had been fools to surrender.

As it turned out, he was right. One witness to the events that followed wrote: "The citizens of Las Vegas were not inclined in this affair to wait the slow operation of the judicial machinery."

About midnight the following Saturday a large crowd collected on Railroad Avenue. All was orderly and quiet as the men marched two by two toward the county jail. As others joined, the line grew to a half mile in length.

There was no resistance. The jailer promptly handed over the keys, and the three murderers were removed from their cells. Then they were marched to an old windmill tower in the center of the plaza where ropes were waiting.

James West was hauled up first. But somehow he got his hands loose and grabbed the rope above his head. Below young Tom Henry yelled to him, "Can't you see they intend to kill you? Stop your struggles and die like a man." West then dropped his hands and was strangled.

At that moment someone stepped from the crowd and fired a shot into Henry. Afterwards it was said the assailant was Marshal Carson's widow, dressed in male attire, who had acted as one of the mob leaders.

As Henry lay on the ground wounded he cried out, "Boys, give me another in the head." Those

"Hanging Windmill," on the Plaza at Las Vegas, New Mexico, ca. 1879-80. Photo by James N. Furlong. Courtesy Museum of New Mexico. Neg. No. 14386.

were his final words, for about one hundred shots followed. Both men were killed instantly and West's body, dangling from the rope, was also riddled with bullets.

According to press reports, the entire community agreed that justice had been well served. There was only one disquieting fact that occasioned the sentiment of shame. Members of the posse who had made the capture and offered such strong promises of protection had been among the ringleaders of the lynch mob.

The Worst Outlaw

The California frontier had Joaquin Murieta, a Robin Hood- style bandit who relieved the wealthy of their treasure and delivered it into the hands of the impoverished. South Texas had Juan Cortina, declared an outlaw by the state when he raised an army to fight oppression and social injustice.

And New Mexico had Vicente Silva. Unfortunately, he was a desperado and cutthroat of the first order, wholly lacking in the nobility of purpose associated with Murieta or Cortina. In fact, Silva would make some of the godfathers of a later era look like Sunday school teachers by comparison.

He was born to a respectable family near Albuquerque in 1845. Evidently, there was nothing in young Vicente's early career to suggest that he carried poison in his soul. Indeed, afterward he was remembered as a pleasing and sociable youth who inspired respect by his manner. But by then the universal judgment was that, all along, he had been a wolf in sheep's clothing.

In 1875 Vicente Silva moved to Las Vegas, a booming mercantile town which served as the principal supply point for ranches throughout eastern New Mexico and parts of the Texas Panhandle. He opened the Imperial Saloon, a block from the present Old Town Plaza, and began to prosper. In time he added a dance hall and gambling room to the business.

With him to Las Vegas had come his wife Teles-

Vicente Silva (1845-1893) in an 1896 illustration. Courtesy Museum of New Mexico. Neg. No. 143691.

fora and her brother, Gabriel Sandoval, a timid young man who worked in the Imperial as a bartender. Soon Vicente and Telesfora adopted a baby girl, Emma, found abandoned in the manger of a nearby livery stable. She became the pet of the household.

For a while, it appears that Vicente was satisfied with the profits from his saloon, reputed to be the largest in the territory. But by the late 1880s, his hunger for money had turned him toward a life of crime. Back rooms of the Imperial became headquarters for a large gang of rustlers and robbers, all of whose activities were masterminded by proprietor Silva.

Over the next five years, while he remained outwardly respectable, his men carried out dozens of hideous crimes. Cattle stolen from as far east as the Texas line were driven to Silva's secret ranch at Monte Largo (between Albuquerque and Santa Fe) where the brands were either altered or the animals were slaughtered and the meat sold at the mining camp of San Pedro.

No merchant or other businessman in northeastern New Mexico known to possess ready cash was safe from attack by thugs of the Silva band. Among those murdered and robbed were storekeepers Jacob Stuzman and Abraham Aboulofia, a Syrian, and Carpio Salas, treasurer of the public school board.

Territorial and San Miguel County officials tried to end the violence, but their investigations met dead ends. Vicente Silva covered his tracks well. From gang members he exacted oaths of loyalty and secrecy. And three of his best men were members of the Las Vegas Municipal Police Force. Few in town dared oppose him.

Then Silva made a mistake. He ordered some of his men to steal cattle from the ranch of José Esquibel, fifty miles south of Las Vegas. Esquibel was not the sort to take his loss lying down. From Patricio Maes, one of the gang with whom he was acquainted, he learned that the rustled stock had been driven to Monte Largo. With some of his cowboys, Esquibel went and recovered the cattle. Then he headed for Las Vegas to swear out a warrant in District Court against Vicente Silva.

At last the outlaw leader was exposed. Leaving the Imperial Saloon in the hands of a nephew, he fled to a hideout in the mountains near Mora. Often though, he would sneak back into Las Vegas under cover of darkness and from his old office direct the continuing activities of the crime ring.

Becoming a fugitive seems to have made Vicente Silva more vicious and bloodthirsty than ever. He carried a special grudge for Patricio Maes who had betrayed him to the rancher Esquibel.

Late one winter's night, while a blizzard howled outside, Silva summoned all of his confederates to a meeting in the saloon. He announced that Maes, who had been dragged in, would be tried as a traitor. A mock court was arranged and a jury of outlaws selected. Patricio Maes pleaded innocent and pledged loyalty to the gang and its leader.

Half the jury was ready to believe him. But Vicente Silva, disliking the way things were going, brought in a keg of whiskey. A half hour later, the drunk jurors voted unanimously for a guilty verdict and prompt execution.

Carrying their victim down the deserted and snow-choked street, the necktie party reached an iron bridge over the narrow Gallinas River. After giving Maes a brief moment to utter a prayer, the men tied a noose around his neck and the other end to the bridge girder. Then they tossed him off into space. Next morning, Las Vegas residents found the frozen body swinging in the winter wind.

Telesfora Silva, although she knew about her husband's criminal activities, herself remained an honest person. When Vicente fled to the hills, she opened a lunch counter in Las Vegas to provide for her own support and that of little Emma.

Vicente Silva, perhaps consumed by blood lust or madness, decided that his wife and her brother

Gabriel were plotting to turn him over to the authorities. By a ruse, he lured the unsuspecting Gabriel to a deserted cemetery, stabbed him in the heart, and threw his body into the garbage dump.

Then he sent a note to Telesfora, instructing her to slip out of Las Vegas unseen and come to the outlaw camp in the mountains. Once there, he accused her of treachery and also stabbed her to death.

With that horrible deed, however, some of his men decided that they had had enough. Telesfora had been a favorite among them and they plotted revenge.

When their leader called them to come and remove his wife's body, they acted promptly. Wrapping Telesfora in a blanket, they carried her to a nearby arroyo. Vicente himself jumped on an overhanging bank of earth until a piece broke away and buried the corpse.

Chuckling to himself, Silva turned and started back toward camp. At that point, his henchman, Antonio Valdez, came up behind him, placed a pistol at the back of his head, and pulled the trigger. Vicente Silva, the scourge of Las Vegas and the terror of the countryside, fell dead. It was May 18, 1893.

With the leader gone, the Silva gang quickly fell apart. Some of the desperados were hung from telephone poles by Las Vegas vigilantes. Others, in more legal fashion, were sentenced to the gallows by the courts. A few, by turning evidence against their fellows got off with long sentences in the penitentiary. The last surviving member of the gang died in 1940.

And what of little Emma Silva after the death of

her adoptive parents in 1893? She was raised by friends until her marriage at age nineteen. A few years after the wedding, her clothes caught fire while she was standing in front of an open fireplace. Eleven days later, she died from the burns. The hand of fate, it would seem, was turned against all who had any connection with Vicente Silva.

Black Jack

Clayton in the far northeastern corner of New Mexico possesses little in the way of tourist attractions. But the town does boast the grave of train robber Thomas "Black Jack" Ketchum. It is located in the center of the municipal cemetery.

Without a doubt the hanging of Black Jack in 1901 was the most celebrated event in Clayton's history. A photographer was on hand for the occasion and made a series of startling pictures.

Copies of these pictures are on display today in the bar of Clayton's Ecklund Hotel. They have been published many times in popular outlaw books. The most grisly of the lot shows the body of the outlaw with his head cradled under his arm.

You see, no one in Clayton had ever performed a hanging before, and several mistakes were made. For one, the rope was not properly stretched beforehand. For another, nobody thought to measure the condemned man to be sure his feet would clear the ground (in fact they hit bottom when the trap was sprung).

And finally, no account was taken of Black

Hanging of "Black Jack" Ketchum, Clayton, New Mexico, April 26, 1901. Photo by John Wheatley Studio. Courtesy Museum of New Mexico. Neg. No. 128886.

Jack's heavy weight. The result was that when he hit the end of the rope, he was decapitated. Onlookers first realized that when they noticed blood gushing from under the black hood that had been put over his head.

After time was allowed for local folk to pose with the headless corpse and have their pictures made, the undertaker was brought in to put things right. He sewed the head to the torso and the body was placed in a pine box. Burial followed in Boot

Hill on the outskirts of town, where the less-desirable were banished.

What had brought Thomas Ketchum to this well-publicized and admittedly deserved end? The answer is simple: a career in crime and a wasted life.

It all started back in San Saba County, Texas, where Tom was born in 1863. In his youth, he and his brother Sam worked as cowboys first in west Texas, then in eastern New Mexico. It is known that they went on several trail drives.

In 1895 the brothers killed fellow Texan John Powers, and that put them permanently on the wrong side of the law. Fleeing to New Mexico they got jobs on the famous Bell Ranch north of Tucumcari. But shortly they held up a nearby store and lit out for the Pecos with a posse hot on their heels.

The posse ran into an ambush and two of its members died. Tom and Sam got away without a scratch. Soon they put together a gang and began holding up trains across the Southwest.

In 1896 another outlaw, Black Jack Christian, was slain in Arizona. Someone mistakenly identified the body as that of Thomas Ketchum. The error was later discovered when Tom robbed a train in northeastern New Mexico. After that folks started calling him Black Jack, mainly because he did resemble the dead Christian.

The last robbery was a solo job, since Sam had been gunned down by a posse a few weeks before and the gang had broken up. Black Jack bungled things badly, taking a shotgun blast in the right arm from the train's conductor.

He was captured, brought to trial, and sentenced to hang in Clayton. Rumor had it that friends would try to rescue him. But as he climbed the steps to the gallows, there was no disturbance among the crowd of spectators. It was clear that he had no friends.

As was customary, the condemned man made a final speech. He declared, "My advice to the boys of the country is not to steal horses or sheep but either rob a train or bank when you get to be an outlaw, and every man who comes in your way, kill him; spare him no mercy, for he will show you none."

Those were scarcely words to win sympathy. Evidently Black Jack's evil reputation was wholly justified.

According to what can be learned in Clayton, Ketchum's coffin was dug up in 1933 and moved to the new town cemetery. For many years the grave was left unmarked. But not long ago a new headstone was installed, so now visitors can easily find it.

Recently, two ladies from Oregon came to town. They claimed to be great-granddaughters of Sam Ketchum, and they had driven down to see Tom's grave.

"Growing up," they said, "it was whispered we had outlaws in our ancestry, but no one in the family would speak about it. This is our first visit to Clayton and we are surprised to learn that everyone knows the Ketchum story here. It's really been eye-opening."

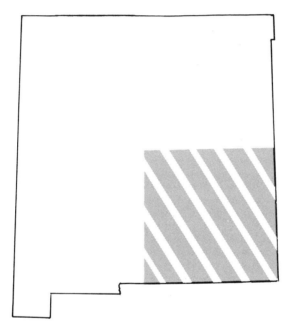

NEW MEXICO

"Paddy" Graydon's Tragic End

Because of two brief incidents in his life—one comic and the other tragic—Captain James "Paddy" Graydon made a small mark on the history of New Mexico in the year 1862.

He's first heard of operating a saloon at Fort Buchanan, Arizona, in the late 1850s. There he was known as a fearless man with a gun who could always be counted upon to lead a posse against hostile Indians.

When the Civil War broke out, Graydon found that southern Arizona was not a safe place for a strong Union man like himself. Confederate sympathizers were everywhere. So, he moved to upper New Mexico where Federal forces were in control.

Soon, with the rank of captain, he was serving in the army as head of a spy company. "Spy" was the term then used for men who at a later day were called "scouts."

Paddy Graydon and his company were inside Fort Craig below Socorro when on February 20, 1862, General H. H. Sibley's Confederate army from El Paso put in an appearance. The fort commander, Colonel Edward Canby, watched the rebels go into camp on the other side of the Rio Grande. He knew that if they decided to attack, he would have a rough go of it, since many of his men were untrained volunteers, native New Mexican farmers.

Graydon, too, had assessed their situation, and he came up with a bizarre plan he hoped would do the Confederates considerable harm at small cost. With Colonel Canby's approval, he got two worn-out mules and loaded a dozen live howitzer shells on their backs. Aided by three of his men, he crossed the river under cover of darkness and stole quietly toward the rebel campfires. At the last moment, he lighted the fuses on the shells and lashed the mules into a run toward the enemy.

Paddy and his companions sped back toward the fort expecting any moment to hear a giant explosion rock the rebel position. But what they heard instead—the clatter of hoofs behind them—chilled their bones to the marrow.

The mules, not liking their abandonment, had turned tail and were trying to catch up. Later, when they told the story, the men would chuckle in merriment. But Captain Graydon at that point saw nothing funny in their predicament.

The retreat became a mad race with the spies applying the spur furiously and the poor mules falling farther behind under the heavy burden of sputtering shells. The men had just reached the shelter of the walls when a thunderous boom rose from the sandy plain outside.

It had been a narrow squeak for Paddy Graydon. In his official report of the incident, Colonel Canby listed total casualties as two mules.

Graydon's name crops up several times in the military records during the next two months, showing that he remained in the thick of the campaign. In April, he was at the Battle of Peralta just below Albuquerque when the Confederate invaders were sent reeling down river toward El Paso.

With the end of the rebel threat, Paddy Graydon was stationed at Fort Stanton near modern Ruidoso. He was placed in command of Volunteer Company H and sent to chase Mescalero Apaches in the surrounding mountains. Colonel Kit Carson was the post commander.

If the scant information we have is correct, Graydon was something of an "Indian hater." That would explain an ugly deed he committed soon after arriving at Fort Stanton. While on patrol, he lured several Apaches to his camp, got them drunk on a keg of whiskey, and then shot them down in cold blood.

That raised the anger of army surgeon J. M. Whitlock. He wrote an indignant letter to a Santa Fe newspaper exposing the crime and identifying Graydon as the culprit.

The two men met one day at the post hospital and exchanged fighting words. Graydon claimed that the doctor was guilty of libelous slander. Whitlock replied that he could prove every word in his letter to the Santa Fe paper. The Captain then proposed a duel, and his challenge was promptly accepted.

He went to his tent to get a gun. When he returned, the pair, without waiting for the usual courtesies associated with formal duels, began blazing away at each other.

Paddy Graydon got off one shot, just as his opponent fired. The bullet struck him near the heart. His own shot hit the doctor in the wrist, smashing his pistol at the same time. Whitlock went

Gravestone of Captain James "Paddy" Graydon, National Cemetery, Santa Fe, 1990. Photo by Mary Powell.

straight to the sutler's store, took a shotgun from the rack, loaded it, and waited.

Meanwhile, Graydon's Company H men picked up their fallen leader and carried him to his tent where he died in a matter of minutes. Enraged, they grabbed weapons and hurried onto the parade ground in search of Dr. Whitlock.

Hearing a noisy throng approaching the store, the doctor slipped out the back. But he was felled by a bullet almost at once. The soldiers threw his body into a ditch and used it for target practice.

The disturbance threw the fort into an uproar. Much too late, Kit Carson ordered out the other troops and had them arrest and disarm Company H.

Whitlock had been his personal friend, and no one could recall seeing the normally mild-mannered Kit in such a towering rage. His fury mounted when an examination showed that the doctor had been struck by 130 bullets.

There are two accounts of what happened next. According to one, Kit Carson shouted at Company H, "I'll have you scoundrels swing before sunset."

Another version is given by J. E. Farmer who wrote his recollections of the affair more than fifty years later. He claims that Colonel Carson had the guilty men stand in line and count off, telling them that every fourth one would be immediately shot.

In either case, Kit was soon calmed by his junior officers, who convinced him to let the courts settle the matter. Three of the ring leaders were soon sent to Albuquerque to be tried for murder. But a few days before the trial, members of Company H who had deserted from Fort Stanton broke them out of jail. All then fled to Chihuahua and were not seen again on this side of the border.

Hot-tempered Paddy Graydon not only came to an inglorious end; his name continues to hover like a black cloud over the territorial history of New Mexico.

The Killing of Robert Casey

Justice was neither sure nor swift on the southwestern frontier. The land was so big and offered such an abundance of natural hideouts that criminals routinely escaped punishment. When one happened to be collared, therefore, there were loud demands to make an example of him. That was the case with the murderer of Robert Casey.

In 1867 Casey had come to New Mexico from Texas and bought a ranch on the Rio Hondo between Roswell and Lincoln. Here he ran cattle, operated a grist mill, and raised his family. Rustlers made off with much of his stock, using a running iron to alter his K C brand to a B O brand. But he fought back, eventually prospered, and became a leading figure in those parts.

Robert Casey's untimely death occurred on August 2, 1875. On that date he was attending a county convention in the town of Lincoln, called by a group of reform-minded citizens. It seems they were up in arms against the business firm of Murphy, Riley, and Dolan, which formed the backbone of a political machine that ran local affairs.

At the meeting Casey spoke up strongly against the machine and urged the organization of a citizens' ticket to oppose the county power structure. His proposal was greeted with warm applause.

The meeting adjourned at noon. Two hours later as Casey walked down Lincoln's main street a man named William Wilson shot him from behind an adobe wall. One bullet struck Casey in the face, another in the side. He was killed instantly.

According to what one of Robert Casey's sons (who lived until 1946) related long afterward, the killer had been paid by members of the machine. They had a getaway horse standing by. But one of those on the inside of the plot panicked, jumped on the horse, and left the country. Thus Wilson was stranded afoot and was quickly captured.

He was lodged in the jail at nearby Fort Stanton until his trial the following October. Rumor had it that the men who engineered the crime promised Wilson they would get him off. But feeling was running high, and citizens were in no mood to let a wanton killer loose.

At the trial Wilson claimed that he had shot Casey over a dispute involving an eight-dollar debt. But no one believed that for a minute. Casey's stand on behalf of reform had got him killed without a doubt. Says one writer, "Whatever the cause,this brutal slaying in the heart of the town outraged the public to such a degree that Wilson would have been lynched had not powerful interests in Lincoln intervened to protect him."

The accused was speedily convicted of murder in the first degree and sentenced to hang. His friends made a strong appeal to Territorial Governor Samuel Axtell to commute the sentence. The governor, however, declined to intervene and gave word for the execution to go ahead.

What followed was the first legal hanging in Lincoln County. As it turned out it proved to be a horrible bungle, producing what one newspaper of the day called a "double hanging."

On the appointed morning carpenters were up early hammering and sawing at the construction of the gallows. For several hours spectators—men, women and children—streamed in from the surrounding countryside. A hanging was a notable occasion, not to be missed.

At eleven o'clock the condemned man arrived in an army ambulance escorted by soldiers from the

Lincoln County Courthouse, Lincoln, New Mexico.
Courtesy Museum of New Mexico. Neg. No. 11634.

fort. He was wearing black funeral clothes. Before
mounting the platform, Wilson shook hands with
several friends. All witnesses described him as calm
and collected.

On the scaffold the death warrant was read in
both English and Spanish. A priest administered the
last rites. A hood was placed over the prisoner's
head and he waited with hands tied.

What happened next was described by a
reporter sent down from the *Santa Fe New Mexican*. "The sheriff descended from the scaffold and

in an instant justice so long outraged was avenged, and the perpetrator of one of the foulest murders which had ever disgraced a civilized community was no more."

The reference to "instant justice" was not quite accurate as the reporter himself went on to explain. "After hanging 9½ minutes the body was cut down and placed in the coffin, when it was discovered that life was not yet extinct. A rope was then fastened around his neck and the crowd drew the body from the coffin and suspended it from the gallows where it hung for twenty minutes longer. It was then cut down and placed in the coffin and buried."

That's what was meant by a "double hanging." The late historian William Keleher referred to the incident as "reflecting life in the raw in a frontier community."

The Outlaw As Lawman

During the 1880s the Southwest's leading cities were struggling toward respectability, trying to live down an image of lawlessness that most Easterners had of them. Nevertheless, places like El Paso, Tucson, and Denver still experienced occasional outbursts of gunplay in the streets, reminiscent of the worst Wild West cowtowns.

According to a journalist of the era, New Mexico's chief municipality could claim top honors in the "wildness" category. He proclaimed: "All western towns are vicious but none of them flaunt their

Railroad [Central] Avenue, Albuquerque, New Mexico, ca. 1880. Courtesy Museum of New Mexico. Neg. No. 148301.

vice so openly in the faces of strangers as Albu-querque."

One of those strangers who was able to confirm the journalist's observations was Lieutenant John G. Bourke. Going through Albuquerque on the train in April of 1881, he descended from his car during a short layover.

"At the moment of stepping upon the plat-form," he records, "two high-toned gentlemen of the town were blazing away with pistols at each other farther up the street." And he added with seeming regret, "Unfortunately, neither was killed!"

It was just that sort of episode that prompted

civic leaders to fund a merchant police force and hire the first town marshal. The man who got the job proved to be an unlikely rogue going by the assumed name of Milt Yarberry.

He owned a shady reputation, having been chased out of Canon City, Colorado, for operating a dishonest saloon. But Milt was known to be quick with his guns and that qualification, it seems, took precedence over his moral failings.

The town fathers, however, soon had to question their wisdom in hiring such a man. The first serious incident occurred on March 27, 1881.

Apparently Marshal Yarberry held a grudge against a fellow named Harry Brown, son of a former Tennessee governor. Both men shared the attentions of a pretty widow, Sadie Preston.

On the evening in question, Yarberry called his rival into an alley, they argued over Sadie, and it ended with the marshal pulling a gun and pumping four shots into Brown. At once he turned himself in to County Sheriff Perfecto Armijo.

At a preliminary hearing, Yarberry claimed self-defense. Although no gun had been found on the victim, casting suspicion on the plea, the marshal was acquitted.

In territorial society, most men in fact carried arms. As a popular saying had it, "A six-shooter went with every pair of pants." Local custom dictated that firearms must be worn or carried in plain view. And upon entering a saloon, the universal rule required guns to be checked with the bartender. The feeling then was that if Brown had not carried a pistol, it was his own fault.

On the following June 18, Yarberry was involved

in a second fatal episode, and this time he did not escape the consequences. He was patrolling the streets when the sound of a shot was heard.

"Who's firing?" he demanded to know. Someone pointed to Charles Campbell, who had the misfortune to be strolling by at that moment.

Milt Yarberry whipped out his pistol and shot the man dead. According to witnesses, he gave a little dance and shouted gleefully, "I've downed the S___ o___ B_____!"

The town marshal again entered a plea of self-defense, but now it failed to hold water. He was convicted of murder after a trial in May 1882 and sentenced to hang.

Some one hundred Albuquerqueans, hoping to speed the course of justice, assembled one evening in a livery stable and laid plans for a lynching. Sheriff Armijo got wind of the meeting, fearlessly barged in, and forced the crowd to back down.

Yarberry's attorney made an appeal to the Territorial Supreme Court and, while it was being decided, the condemned man was lodged in the Santa Fe jail. The Court upheld the conviction and sentence.

Early on the morning of February 9, 1883, Yarberry was herded aboard a special railroad car and sent back to Albuquerque under heavy guard. At the depot he was met by a mob of curious spectators and an escort of state militia. Loaded on a street railway car, Milt made his last ride to the county jail.

Scores of citizens had been sent engraved invitations to the hanging, and others, not so favored, paid as much as a dollar for standing room on nearby rooftops. Instead of the solemn mood one might have expected from the crowd, an almost carnival-like atmosphere prevailed.

Still protesting that he had killed only in self-defense, the marshal was led to a special hanging device modeled after plans published in a recent issue of the *Scientific American*. A black hood and noose were fitted over his head, and as a 400-pound lead weight dropped, he was hauled into the air, or "Jerked to Jesus," as the press bluntly put it.

The body was carried to the Santa Barbara cemetery and buried with the rope still in place. Milt Yarberry's hanging was the first and last execution of a peace officer in the New Mexico Territory.

Reflections on Billy the Kid

One subject that never seems to lose its appeal for readers around the world is the life of Billy the Kid. Probably no other early-day New Mexican is so well known.

A wealthy lady from Roswell was traveling in the Far East a few years ago. While she was on a cruise ship in the South China Sea, her Oriental cabin boy learned she was from New Mexico. The first thing he wanted to hear was stories about Billy the Kid.

At this late date, and after the publication of so many books, it is practically impossible to say anything new about the troubles in Lincoln County. But that doesn't mean, of course, that the final word has been written.

Far from it! Practically every phase of the bloody war and almost every aspect of the Kid's part in it remain subjects of controversy. So arguments will persist over who killed who. . .and why. And, magazine editors will continue to print stories that rehash the smallest details because they know there's a readership for such things.

The first point is that authors can't write about Billy the Kid and remain neutral. It seems you have to accept him either as a murdering young punk with no redeeming qualities or as a romantic Robin Hood figure, decent by nature, who was driven to a life of crime by chance and circumstance.

There is no middle ground. At least it so appears in the huge body of literature that has accumulated since the Kid's death at the hands of Pat Garrett, more than one-hundred years ago.

At the very beginning, one encounters questions over Billy's true name. Was he born William Bonney or Henry McCarty? He used both at various stages of his life, together with other assorted aliases.

And where was he born? The majority of authors say Brooklyn. But towns in Indiana, Ohio, Kansas, and even New Mexico have also been suggested. On source claims that the Kid first saw the light of day in Limerick, Ireland. We will probably never know for certain.

Perhaps the most famous statement about Billy is that "he killed a man for each of the 21 years that he lived." The quote was recorded by young Susan Wallace, wife of Governor Lew Wallace. She claims that the Kid himself made that boast. If true, he may have intended it as a macabre joke.

The fact is, Billy the Kid, handy as he was with a pistol, slew far fewer than twenty-one men. The late authority on outlaws, Ramon F. Adams, studied the matter closely and decided that the actual number was probably six. Three others were possible, involving mass gunfights in which the Kid was one of many participants.

Adams concludes that it is highly unlikely Billy was the man who killed Sheriff William Brady, although he was a member of the ambush party which gunned down the lawman and his deputy on the streets of Lincoln. But it was for the murder of Brady that the young outlaw went to trial in Mesilla and was sentenced to hang.

Lodged in the Lincoln County Courthouse a-waiting execution, Billy the Kid made his celebrated escape on April 28, 1881. That incident, involving the shooting of two deputies, created a sensation at the time.

A question left for historians was, how did the Kid obtain the gun used to blast his way to freedom. Now it is believed that a friend hid a six-shooter in the outdoor privy and Billy slipped it in his shirt when he was escorted out back.

With that gun, he shortly killed Deputy James Bell and then taking a shotgun he felled Deputy Bob Olinger. Sheriff Pat Garrett had left the pair in charge that day while he rode to White Oaks to purchase lumber for Billy's gallows.

The young outlaw said afterward that he much regretted the death of Bell, an affable fellow with whom he'd played cards during his brief captivity. But Deputy Olinger was another matter.

Throughout Lincoln County, Bob Olinger had been feared and hated. He was a vicious man who had killed three persons in cold blood. Even his

William Brady (1825-1878), sheriff of Lincoln County, New Mexico. Courtesy Museum of New Mexico. Neg. No. 105103.

boss, Sheriff Garrett, was afraid of him. When folks asked Garrett why he kept the deputy on, he could only reply that men willing to take the job were scarce.

While Billy was locked in the courthouse, Olinger had taken special delight in taunting him. He often said he hoped the Kid would try to escape so that he could have the pleasure of putting a bullet in him.

After the breakout, young Susan McSween chanced to meet Olinger's mother and, out of courtesy, expressed sympathy over the death of her son. She was greatly shocked when the old woman replied, "Bob was a murderer from the cradle and if there is a hell, I know he is in it."

Susan was the widow of Alexander McSween, who died in the Lincoln County War. Billy the Kid had been on her husband's side, and she came to know him well.

In her judgment, "Billy was not half as bad as his enemies, who were determined to kill him. He was neither a bad man nor a murderer and did not kill wantonly; most of those he shot richly deserved it."

Hers perhaps was a somewhat prejudiced view. But not that of Territorial Governor Miguel Otero. He met the youthful outlaw while he was held briefly in the Santa Fe city jail. Years afterward, Governor Otero wrote that, upon studying all the facts surrounding the war in Lincoln County, it was his opinion that, "Billy the Kid sinned less than he was sinned against."

Wild Days in White Oaks

Did you ever have the notion that you'd like to live in a ghost town? The few folks who reside in the old mining camp of White Oaks, in a small valley northeast of Carrizozo, will tell you that it beats modern city life any day of the year.

As far as prosperity goes, the town has seen better times. The mines and main business houses have long been closed. But what remains is a picturesque setting, untainted air, and silence—things that are hard to come by today.

The place, named for nearby White Oaks Spring, got its start in 1879. Three men prospecting for placer gold sat down on a hillside to eat their lunch. Afterward one of them climbed up a ridge to survey the country and stumbled upon an outcrop of shiny metal.

Since he was on the dodge from the law, he couldn't stick around to profit from his discovery. So he sold out to his two companions for a pair of boots, a jug of whiskey, and forty dollars. The mine that he sold for this paltry sum later yielded several hundred thousand dollars in ore.

In the 1880s White Oaks became a boom town. Other mines opened, shacks and tents sprouted overnight, and the saloon keepers and gamblers moved in. One notorious character of those early days was Madam Varnish.

She hit town with three charming daughters and a yen to find a husband who would take care of the whole family. The treasurer from a neighboring county, in White Oaks on business, fell in love with the widow and promised to marry her and support the daughters.

Off to Roswell they went by stagecoach to tie the knot. Madam Varnish soon returned but without the bridegroom. He appeared a few days later and had her arrested.

The charge? She had stolen $3,500 from under his pillow on their wedding night!

Madam Varnish was never brought to trial. Local gossips claimed that she threatened to reveal in court that her new husband had stolen the money from the county till. He quietly left White Oaks and the matter ended.

With her stake of $3,500, Madam opened a gambling hall and saloon called the Little Casino. She dealt faro with a swift hand while her daughters waited on tables and smiled at the customers.

The family business prospered even though competition was tough from other saloons. One rival was the Star Saloon and Opera House, which provided a stage for big-time traveling performers.

Liquor was easy to find, but religion was not. Some of the more solid townsfolk began to think of a church. Until one was built, they agreed to meet in a saloon which had plenty of floor space.

The first service was to begin with the singing of "The Old Rugged Cross," but nobody knew the words. Since everyone was familiar with "Old Black Joe" and "Swanee River" they were rung in as substitutes.

By the 1890s some four thousand people had settled in White Oaks and new buildings gave the town

White Oaks, New Mexico. Courtesy Museum of New Mexico. Neg. No. 55358.

an air of permanence. There were banks, newspapers, and large stores which supplied the miners in the surrounding Jicarilla Mountains. Plush hotels offered lodging to visiting mine speculators and a rendezvous for local cattlemen.

Some famous names were seen on White Oaks' streets in those boom days after 1880. Billy the Kid is supposed to have met and conferred with Territorial Governor Lew Wallace in one of the hotels.

Renowned western novelist Emerson Hough (author of *The Covered Wagon*) was a resident for several years and used the mining camp for the setting of one of his many books. William McDonald,

New Mexico's first governor after statehood, began his law career in an office in the Exchange Bank on White Oaks Avenue.

Just before the turn of the century, the Santa Fe and the El Paso and Northwestern railroads were rumored to be laying tracks toward White Oaks. That set off a new round of speculation fever.

But in the end, both lines by-passed the town, sounding its death knell. The mines closed down one by one, and a new ghost town was born.

Trouble in Phoenix

Everyone knows that Phoenix is in Arizona. But few people are aware that New Mexico once had a Phoenix of its own. Located a mile south of the town of Eddy (now Carlsbad) in the Pecos Valley, Phoenix was a wild, untamed place, famous as a rendezvous for outlaws.

Eddy was the creation of the Pecos Irrigation and Improvement Company, which in 1890 was busily developing 24,000 acres of farmland and building McMillan and Avalon dams. The company also built the Pecos Valley Railway, nicknamed "The Pear Vine," running from Pecos, Texas, and ending at Eddy.

The founders of Eddy, being upstanding businessmen, wanted a quiet and sober town. So, from the beginning they outlawed the sale of liquor. However, the flood of workers who had come to construct the huge irrigation canal and the dams wanted a place where they could drink and let off steam.

To cater to their desires, a lawless element arrived and established Phoenix. S. T. Roberts, a prominent Eddy merchant, described it this way: "Phoenix had a population of about 900 people. Their chief industry was gambling, liquor, and wild women resorts. It was a hell of a town, a mecca for all the underworld of the Southwest."

Not much could be done in the way of keeping order. The county sheriff, Dave Kemp, was a partner of Ed Lyle, who ran the biggest and bawdiest saloon in Phoenix. Honest citizens of Eddy were at a loss as to how to put a bridle on the activities of their wild neighbors.

Then a local shoot-out brought Dee Harkey to their attention. He was a young man of steady habits who had recently arrived from Texas and taken over management of the local meat market in Eddy.

One day a gambler from Phoenix, George High, walked into the market and complained that his wife had been denied credit to purchase pork chops. An argument ensued and he pulled a gun on Harkey. In the shooting that followed, Harkey disarmed his rowdy customer, marched him to the railway station, and forced him to leave the country.

Shortly, a delegation of citizens approached Harkey. Long afterward in his memoirs, he wrote, "They informed me that their county officials were a bunch of crooks, gamblers, and saloon men, and they wanted me to serve as deputy U.S. marshal." The citizens promised to get him the appointment and also put up the large bond required, if only he would take the job.

Now, Dee Harkey had been weaned on the Texas frontier, and he had a bit of experience at Indian fighting and law enforcement. But that made him all the more cautious. So, he asked the citizens

Daniel R. (Dee) Harkey, New Mexico peace officer, 1893-1911. Photo from his autobiography, *Mean as Hell: The Life of a New Mexico Lawman* (1948; reprint, Ancient City Press, 1989), where it appears following page 192 with the caption: "D. R. (Dee) Harkey, who has been shot at more times than any man in the world not engaged in war."

specifically what they wanted him to do in Phoenix.

The leader of the group said, "Well, you know that Phoenix is filled up with saloons, gamblers, and prostitutes. Those women will come out naked when we drive by and they'll get right up in our buggies. We dare not drive through with our families or a prospective buyer for any of our valley land. So if you will just keep those women off the streets when they're naked and out of our buggies, we will be satisfied."

"It dawned on me that anybody ought to be able to do that without having any serious trouble," Harkey wrote later. But just to make sure he rode down to Phoenix. There he called a town meeting in Ed Lyle's saloon and announced that he was considering taking the marshal's job with an eye to cleaning up the place.

Lon Bass, one of Lyle's hired killers, stood up and said that if Harkey took the job and got in their way, he would be gunned down. "Their attitude settled the question of my taking the job," Harkey notes. Never one to run from a fight, he told the Eddy folks he was their man.

After his appointment, he deputized two friends and went to Phoenix in the middle of the night. The prostitutes had rows of little shacks behind the saloons. One by one he entered and arrested the couples he found. By morning he had sixteen couples in the Eddy jail, charged with adultery.

The next night he bagged sixteen more. All were put on the train and sent via El Paso to Socorro, seat of the District Court. By the second day, Phoenix began to notice that some of its citizens and ladies of the evening were missing. When the cause became known, Lon Bass was sent to put a bullet in Dee Harkey.

Dee was waiting in Eddy when he arrived. At his side was sixty-eight-year-old Judge Freeman, carrying a Winchester. When Bass saw that, he turned around and went home. He didn't want to run the risk of killing a judge.

Over the next several years, Harkey kept the pressure on the unruly residents of Phoenix. Finally, Ed Lyle declared he had enough; his business was ruined and he was moving all his equipment and "staff" to Arizona.

On the last morning he loaded a string of freight wagons and buggies with his ladies carrying parasols. On top of the lead wagon rode his fourteen-piece band with instruments at the ready. As the colorful caravan rumbled down Eddy's main street, the band began playing what they called, "Dee Harkey's March." The ladies in the rear sang in chorus, "Farewell, Dee Harkey, farewell!"

With Lyle and his crew gone, Phoenix was abandoned and soon fell into ruin. Harkey went on to serve other jobs as peace officer, finally retiring in 1911.

Apache Justice

If the white men who did battle with them are to be believed, the old-time Apaches were about the best fighters the world has ever seen. Their abilities as warriors were enhanced by almost unlimited physical endurance. And they could follow a track through desert or mountains that was practically invisible to anyone else.

In 1908 a group of Mescalero Apaches demonstrated that despite more than thirty years confinement to a reservation in south-central New Mexico they had not lost their touch.

The incident which brought the Apache warriors out of retirement began on a bitterly cold day in January. Roy McLane, foreman of the Flying H Ranch, rode into the Sacramento Mountains looking for some of his stray cattle. Toward evening, he found tracks leading through a pasture gate not far from the Mescalero Indian Agency.

It was too late to continue the search, so he headed back to headquarters at Elk Spring, fourteen miles away. Next morning, McLane sent his eighteen-year-old brother, Don, to find the missing animals.

The boy was a first rate cowhand, so the prospect of a thirty-mile or more ride that wintry day looked routine. About noon, he stopped by the trader's store at the Mescalero Agency where he spoke briefly with Percy Bigmouth, an Indian youth who worked there.

Continuing on the trail, Don soon realized that the lost cattle were not wandering but were being driven. It appeared that a bit of rustling was afoot. Mid-afternoon he waved at Paul Blazer as he rode past the Blazer gristmill in Tularosa Canyon. That was the last anyone saw of Don McLane alive.

When his brother failed to return that night, Roy grew concerned. It was too cold to be camping out, so surely the boy must have gotten into trouble.

Next morning he saddled up and went looking.

He rode until night overtook him, then he started again on the following day. Finally, he found the tracks of Don's horse in the snow, clearly identified by the long heels on the shoes which Roy himself had earlier nailed on. But there were also the prints of an unshod horse and both sets led westward away from the Mescalero Agency.

Tracking along a steep ridge, Roy McLane came to the carcass of one of his cows, partially butchered. Just beyond he found his brother. He'd been shot through the head and the body was frozen stiff.

Back at the Agency, Roy notified Indian Superintendent James Carroll, who promptly sent word to Sheriff H. M. Denny in Alamogordo. And the manhunt began.

At once, Carroll summoned the Mescalero leaders and asked their help in identifying the killer. Shortly they returned with a full account of the crime.

A deaf and one-eyed Apache named Kit-i-chin had stolen the Flying H cattle. He had been butchering one of them when Don McLane approached from behind. Had he been able to hear the boy coming, he probably would have run away. But knowing he was caught, he snatched up his rifle and shot the cowboy dead.

Feeling was running high among the surrounding ranch folk. Knowing this, the Mescaleros volunteered to form a posse. They were joined by Roy McLane, a deputy sheriff, and a territorial police officer.

The party started down Nogal Canyon, then turned south. Kit-i-chin was heading for Mexico through a maze of steep canyons and rocky ridges.

Mescalero Apache group at the Tertio-Millennial Exposition, Santa Fe, New Mexico, 1883. Photo by Ben Wittick. Courtesy Museum of New Mexico. Neg. No. 56138.

At one point they found the remains of his horse. He had killed it, taken some of the meat for food, and stripped off part of the hide to make moccasins.

The chase lasted for days. The deputy and police officer grew weary, gave up, and left. Only Roy McLane stuck with the Indians.

One afternoon, several of the Mescaleros who had been scouting ahead rushed in and began to speak excitedly in their own language. After a bit, all the Apaches sat down and refused to go any farther.

To all appearances, it was a sit-down strike.

Try as he might, Roy could not get the Indians in motion again. He decided to leave them and ride forty miles to Alamogordo for provisions, which were running low. Perhaps when he returned they would be ready to resume the hunt.

Two days later he was back. The Apaches apparently had not moved. But one of them pointed to a spot on the hillside. Roy McLane climbed up and there sprawled on the ground, riddled with bullets, lay the body of Kit-i-chin.

Only then did he understand the sit-down strike and why the Indians had patiently waited for him to leave for Alamogordo. They wanted no outsider present to witness the final act in the drama. That was the Apache way.

The posse carried Kit-i-chin down to Alamogordo. There they were met by S. S. Ward, owner of the Flying H. The Indians, all twenty of them, spent the night on the floor of the courthouse.

The following morning, Mr. Ward shook hands with the Apaches as they mounted up for the ride back to the Agency. In the hand of each, he placed a twenty-dollar gold piece, as an expression of his gratitude. That was the white man's way.

The Cowboy Detective

For a number of years prior to 1922, one of Santa Fe's most prominent and colorful residents was Charles A. Siringo, popularly known as the "cowboy detective." A small, wiry man, he was friends with practically everyone in town, from the governor to the dogcatcher.

In 1916, New Mexico Governor William C. McDonald persuaded Siringo to accept a commission as a mounted ranger for the state Cattle Sanitary Board. The only thing unusual about that was Charlie Siringo's age, a ripe sixty-one. Undaunted, he saddled up and with a pack horse, he started for his headquarters at Carrizozo in Lincoln County.

His duty was to run down outlaws and stock thieves operating in seven counties north of the Mexican border. Bill Owens, described as a fighting son-of-a-gun, was selected as his partner. As Siringo reported later, "Poor Bill lasted only a short time."

The pair got into a gunfight with cattle thieves at Abo Pass, east of Belen. Owens was shot through the lungs, but he emptied his pistol and killed two of the outlaws before he went down.

"During my two years work as a ranger," said Siringo, "I made many arrests of cattle and horse thieves, and had many close calls, with death staring me in the face." Obviously, Governor McDonald had made a wise choice when he tapped this hard-riding, fast-shooting "senior citizen" for the dangerous ranger job.

Charlie Siringo's career in the West was as adventurous as it was long. Born in Matagorda County, Texas, on the Gulf Coast in 1855, he took to life in the saddle before he was shaving. As he put it, "When I was 12 years of age, in the spring of 1867, I became a full-fledged cowboy, wearing broad sombrero, high-heeled boots, Mexican spurs, and the dignity of a full-grown man."

After trips up the Chisolm Trail and sprees in

the wild cow towns of Kansas, he landed a cowboy job in the Texas Panhandle, still a teen-ager. He fought prairie fires, had run-ins with rustlers, and saw the last herds of buffalo on the Staked Plains.

Mail came to his ranch from Fort Bascom, New Mexico (near present Tucumcari), some two-hundred miles to the west. One day a party of well-armed government surveyors, laying out a mail route, put in an appearance. They were keeping their work a secret, so the cowboys quickly surmised that they were Texas Rangers in disguise.

The next morning, half the crew was gone, having "hit the trail for tall timber in New Mexico and Arizona," as Siringo described it. Many had stolen ranch horses to make their flight. In those days, a significant number of cowboys were on the dodge from the law.

The years drifted by and Charlie Siringo drifted with them. At age thirty, he was tending store in Caldwell, Kansas, and putting in nights writing up his previous experiences on the range. When his book, *A Texas Cowboy*, saw print, its author became famous overnight. Eventually it sold a million copies. Cow country experts have concluded that it was the first autobiography of a cowboy.

Soon after publishing his recollections, Siringo joined the renowned Pinkerton Detective Agency, whose head office was in Chicago. He remained with the firm for two decades, getting in and out of more scrapes than a modern TV sleuth.

The Pinkerton men first gained national fame just before the Civil War when they foiled a plot to assassinate Lincoln on his way to his inauguration. Later they made headlines in trying to break up Jesse

James's gang, an effort that cost several detectives their lives.

Pinkertons were often hired by management as strikebreakers, a chore they carried out so efficiently that they earned the bitter hatred of organized unions. Siringo participated in one piece of such business in Coeur d'Alene, Idaho.

There in 1892 occurred huge labor riots attended by the dynamiting of mines and the murder of managers. In trials that followed, Agent Siringo gave crucial testimony that led to conviction of eighteen union leaders for these crimes. Soon afterward, the home office sent him in pursuit of Butch Cassidy's Wild Bunch.

After leaving the Pinkertons, Charlie Siringo returned to the Southwest and did a good bit of roaming about before settling in Santa Fe. Because of the name he had made in publishing *A Texas Cowboy*, he had access to many persons, on both sides of the law, who were on their way to winning a place in the history books. From them he got firsthand information which he later incorporated in a new book called *Riata and Spurs*.

In that work, the writer had wanted to include some of his own daring adventures while serving with the Pinkertons. But the agency threatened a lawsuit if he revealed any of their professional secrets. So, he had to delete some of his best material.

There is a prominent thoroughfare in Santa Fe today called Siringo Road. But it is a safe bet that not one local resident in five hundred knows for whom it is named.

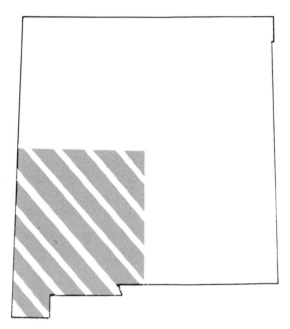

NEW MEXICO

When Scalp Hunting Was a Business

During the decade of the 1830s, the people living along the Mexican border suffered from a particularly bloody spell of Apache raids. The governors of Chihuahua and Sonora, in an effort to stem the tide of destruction, introduced a desperate program. They began offering bounties for Indian scalps.

The plan was intended to curb the deadly raids. But in the end it had the opposite effect. Ruffians and cutthroats from north of the border entered in droves to become scalp hunters, and their activity merely served to inflame the Apaches to new violence.

Most notorious of the bounty men was James Kirker, who in Mexico was known as "Don Santiago" Kirker. Born in Ireland, he had been a privateer on an American ship during the War of 1812, before settling in St. Louis to engage in the grocery business. Finding storekeeping too tame, he left for the Rockies to become a mountain man. He made several trips over the Santa Fe Trail in the 1820s and for a time was an associate of Kit Carson and New Mexico's governor, Manuel Armijo.

At one point Kirker worked for the operators of the Santa Rita copper mines near Silver City. He was responsible for getting pack trains of ore through

Apache camp, San Carlos River, Arizona, ca. 1885.
Photo by Ben Wittick. Courtesy Museum of New Mexico.
Neg. No. 15874.

Apache country to Chihuahua. According to his own claim, he was captured by the Indians and allowed to join the tribe, eventually rising to the rank of war chief. Certain reports credited him with leading war parties against the white men. Both the governors of Chihuahua and New Mexico declared him an outlaw and posted a price on his head.

Don Santiago was as crafty as he was tough. Sending a secret message to Governor Angel Trias in Chihuahua City, he offered to turn against his Indian friends in exchange for a pardon and fifty dollars for every scalp he brought in. The proposal was accepted.

Scouring the frontier, Kirker put together a small army of bounty hunters composed of renegade Shawnee and Delaware Indians and Mexican and American soldiers of fortune. With this force, he swept through the Apache homeland along the border.

His bloodiest success took place in western Chihuahua. There his men encountered a camp of several hundred Apaches who had recently captured a merchant caravan carrying a load of whiskey. Most of the Indians were drunk, so the bounty hunters went among them easily, killing men, women, and children. The Shawnees scalped the victims and salted the grisly trophies to preserve them. Within weeks other camps were overrun and their luckless occupants stripped of their hair.

At the conclusion of the campaign, the blood-stained cavalcade rode toward Chihuahua City to claim its reward. Five miles from the outskirts, Kirker's rogues were met by the governor and his wife in a carriage, a brass band, and hundreds of cheering citizens waving handkerchiefs. They turned over a pack mule loaded with 182 scalps.

That evening Kirker and his companions were guests of honor at a state banquet and grand ball. There was much excitement too because they had brought back a number of Mexican women and children who had been captives of the Apaches.

James Kirker carried out other scalp hunting expeditions. (He called it "barbering.") At the end of his career, he claimed to have drawn bounties on a total of 487 Indian topknots. Over the years, dozens of other men engaged in the gruesome trade, but none were as successful or as infamous as he.

Later in life, Kirker moved to California where he survived a major disaster. On the afternoon of October 29, 1850, the people of San Francisco were holding a celebration marking California's recent admission to the Union. There were parades, fireworks, and speeches.

In the evening Jim Kirker went aboard the new steamboat *Sagamore*, tied up at the waterfront. Planning to take the vessel to his home in Stockton, he was crossing the deck to buy a ticket when the boilers suddenly blew up. About fifty people were killed and many others injured.

As a survivor of the tragedy, Kirker was asked to give his account for a local newspaper. "I—James Kirker was going aft to pay my passage, when the explosion took place, and was thrown some 10 or 15 feet in the air and lit on the bodies of 2 dead persons. I saw 2 persons hanging on the side of the wreck badly wounded and crying for help. I caught and pulled them in.

"I had been in the Rocky Mountains since 1821,

trapping beaver and killing grizzly bears and fighting Apaches. But being blown sky-high by a little hot water is more than I have been accustomed to."

Two years later, Kirker died in bed, it is said, of cancer. His doctor was a cancer specialist whose treatment for the disease was a remedy made of skunk oil.

The Hanging of Russian Bill

A century ago on the New Mexico frontier it was considered bad manners to ask a fellow his name or where he came from. If he didn't volunteer to tell you, then it was none of your business.

A well-known and colorful figure around Lordsburg in the early '80s was a man known only as Russian Bill. He was tall and handsome, with long blond hair in the style of General Custer. He sported a fancy six-gun, wore a white sombrero, and favored large, clanking spurs on his hand-tooled boots. He was what we would call today a "drugstore cowboy." His strong Russian accent gave him his nickname. Exactly where he came from and what his story was, no one knew and no one asked.

Russian Bill liked to play the role of a desperado, though in fact he was a rather mild-mannered gent. Folks around southwestern New Mexico began to suspect that he was not an outlaw at all. This hurt Bill since he figured he was losing esteem. So he went down to Animas near the Arizona line and joined an outlaw gang run by Curly Bill. About all he did was tend cattle the others had stolen and patch

Shakespeare, New Mexico. Courtesy Museum of New Mexico. Neg. No. 55239.

them up when they got shot. Such activities did nothing to enhance his own reputation.

One day he rode up to Shakespeare, just below Lordsburg. There he fell in with a hard case named Sandy King who was wanted for killing a man in Silver City. A fight started and King was captured. But Bill stole a horse and fled eastward on the run. A posse caught him asleep in a boxcar at Deming and brought him back to Shakespeare.

The stories vary as to what happened after that. But the version provided me by Mrs. Rita Hill, foremost authority on the history of Shakespeare, is probably closest to the truth.

According to Mrs. Hill, once in town Russian Bill was taken to the Grant House, a well-known restaurant that also served as a stage station. The townspeople had decided to hang him, since he was guilty of a capital offense—horse stealing. For good measure, they thought it would be appropriate to provide a rope for Sandy King too.

Both men stood solemnly in the dining room and somebody asked, "Where'll we hang 'em?"

The station keeper replied, "Right to those timbers in the ceiling. They won't be the first ones."

A noose was placed over Russian Bill's head, the line was thrown over the main beam, and ten or twelve men hauled him off the floor. The end of the rope was tied to a post, and the crowd stood around and watched until his body quit twitching.

Sandy King had turned pale, watching his pardner swing. Hoping to delay his own end, he said, "Boys, I'd sure like a drink."

Somebody brought him a tin cup of whiskey and he gulped it down. Moments later he was dangling in the air by his neck.

The two bodies were left where they were for the night, the crowd broke up, and the door to the restaurant and station was swung shut.

Early the next morning the stagecoach rolled in and several sleepy-eyed passengers climbed down. They were hungry for breakfast, but when they walked into the dining room they suddenly lost their appetites. There hung Russian Bill and Sandy King.

"What did they hang them for?" one of the pas

sengers asked. "Well, Russian Bill here stole a horse," the keeper answered. "And Sandy King was just a damned nuisance."

A few months later a letter reached the Shakespeare postmaster from a Russian noblewoman asking about her missing son. From the details, it was clear she meant Russian Bill. Jokes were a little rough in the old West, Mrs. Hill says. The postmaster wrote back, "Dear Madam—I'm sorry to report that your son has died of throat trouble."

Joe Fowler Meets His Maker

There are so many versions of the lynching of Joe Fowler that historians are at a loss to say which is the true one. But at least two points are beyond dispute. The first is that the outlaw in question was duly taken from the local jail by the Socorro vigilantes one night in 1883 and was suspended by the neck from what was always known thereafter as "The Hanging Tree." The second inarguable point is that he richly deserved his fate.

Piecing together the conflicting stories, the affair seems to have come about in this way. Joe Fowler was born and raised in Indiana. He was well brought up and possessed of personal charm. But young Joe had a serious flaw. When drinking, he lost control and became mean tempered.

At an early age he emigrated to Texas and entered the cattle business. Of his wife, whom he had brought from Indiana, he was wildly jealous. Coming home unexpectedly one night, he found her consorting with another man. Drawing his pistol Joe Fowler shot him dead.

Soon after, he left for the New Mexico Territory. In Las Vegas he operated a dance hall and eventually married one of the dancers. When he had accumulated a bankroll, Joe moved down to Socorro County and bought a large ranch.

The herds grew and the outfit prospered. But ugly rumors began to surface. It was said that Fowler rustled cattle from his neighbors and that he paid his cowhands next to nothing.

Indeed, one persistent tale claimed that the boss was in the habit of murdering some of his employees at the end of the month to avoid delivering over their wages. True or not, workers at the Fowler ranch had an uncanny way of disappearing.

Then in October 1883 Joe sold his ranch for $52,000 cash. With Mrs. Fowler he rode into the town of Socorro and deposited the money in the bank. Next he visited the office of the *Socorro Chieftain* and told the editor he wanted to place an ad. This was the notice he wrote out on a scrap of paper:

> "I hev muny to pay my detts. Eny I owe kin kum and git it."
>
> —Joe Fowler

The citizens of Socorro were all too familiar with Mr. Fowler's drinking binges, so when he started one now most of them arranged to keep out of his way. A visiting cowboy was told by the town barber that Joe probably murdered thirty or forty people. That was perhaps an exaggeration, but no one could say for sure.

As the evening wore on, Joe Fowler made the round of saloons getting meaner by the hour. And it was not long before he killed a man. The circumstances of the crime vary considerably, according to which account you read.

One writer claims that Joe was in the bar of the the Windsor Hotel and took to shooting at the feet of patrons to make them dance. Hotel proprietor Bob Monroe came up behind him and snatched away his gun, whereupon Fowler spun around and stabbed him to death.

In the version of William French, a prominent rancher, the murder took place in the Grand Hotel, not the Windsor. And the victim was not the proprietor, but rather a traveling salesman who got in Fowler's way and received a mortal knife wound in the stomach.

Perhaps closer to the truth is the story that appeared in the territorial press. The news reports asserted that troublesome Fowler had been arrested for disorderly conduct. As he was being led to jail, a friend of his, Joseph Cale, approached him in the street and spoke to him. Without warning, Joe pulled a knife from his vest and stabbed Cale, who died three days later.

In any event, a murder was committed and Joe Fowler stood trial. Having money in the bank, he hired two slick lawyers, one from Albuquerque and the other from Santa Fe. They argued that their client, being drunk, was not responsible for his actions. But the jury disagreed and found Joe guilty. The judge sentenced him to hang.

His attorneys appealed the verdict to a higher court, and that threw fear into Socorro residents,

Plaza, Socorro, New Mexico, Fourth of July, n.d. Photo by
G. M. Shaw. Courtesy Museum of New Mexico.
Neg. No. 14806.

lest it be overturned. Further, Mrs. Fowler was
rumored to have hired Texas gunmen to free her
husband.

One of the defense attorneys was a young man,
new to New Mexico, Neill B. Field. During the trial
he had spoken eloquently of justice and due process
of law. Afterward, upon hearing that the townsfolk

were considering dealing with his client in their own way, he became alarmed.

"If one hair on Mr. Fowler's head is touched," declared Field with passion, "I will leave Socorro forever."

At that point the Socorro vigilantes took a hand. In the dead of night, some two hundred armed men moved silently toward the jail. They overpowered the guard and dragged out Fowler still wearing the chains by which he had been staked to the dirt floor of his cell. He was yelling, cursing, pleading, and offering bribes. But his doom was sealed.

When he saw there was no escape, he asked to be shot, or else to be allowed to jump from a wall with a rope around his neck. The vigilantes were not in a benevolent frame of mind, however.

Reaching a tree, they tied a noose around the murderer's neck. Then roughly, Joe Fowler was jerked off the ground, and in the colorful speech of the day, "he paid for his crime in the court of Judge Lynch."

The body was left hanging through the next day and three- thousand people are said to have viewed it. A coroner's jury convened and issued a formal ruling on the Fowler demise. It read: "Deceased came to his death at the hands of a mob of unknown persons, who placed a rope around his neck and hanged him until he was dead."

Several years later one of the crowd, recounting the episode, said, "What could we do? After that lawyer threatened to leave Socorro if we took the law into our own hands, we just had to hang Joe Fowler!"

An Outrage in Silver City

The *Silver City Enterprise* was one of the historic newspapers of territorial New Mexico. It was founded in 1882 at a time when a flood of journalists were establishing eight new papers in town. Competition soon drove the others out of business. But not the *Enterprise*. With lively reporting it flourished, and in fact survives to the present day.

During its first years, the paper was preoccupied with news of Indian troubles. But it also had a good deal to say about the desperados who infested the mountains and deserts surrounding Silver City. It seems the neighboring mining camps were a magnet drawing undesirable elements to the area.

A curious case was reported during December of 1884. At that time a pair of outlaws was on trial for murdering three Chinese. The defendants were Abel Duran and Aurilio Lora. Another man charged with the crime, Carlos Chavez, had earlier escaped jail and was killed by lawmen who were trying to recapture him.

Chief witness against Duran and Lora was a ten-year-old boy named Luther Carey, who happened to be deaf and mute. By chance he had wandered away from home and was at the ranch of Ay Way Muck east of town when the crime was committed.

This was actually the second trial. At the first, the defendants had been found guilty and sentenced to death. But in their appeal to the Supreme Court,

Silver City, New Mexico, ca. 1900. Photo by O. C. Hinman.
Courtesy Museum of New Mexico. Neg. No. 142844.

the verdict was overturned and a new trial had been ordered. The reversal came because the boy Luther did not know sign language, and his testimony had been explained by his mother, the only one who could understand the meaning of his nods and gestures.

Subsequently, however, Luther had gone to a school for the deaf in Texas where he mastered sign language. Since he now had the capacity for communication, the alleged murderers were brought to trial once more.

94

Through a sign interpreter, the youngster related what had occurred on the fatal evening of February 3, 1883. It had been nearly dark when he observed five men ride up to Ay Way Muck's tent, which served as the ranch headquarters. Two other Chinese were there besides the owner.

The men on horseback had moved their hands as if asking directions. Then they dismounted and went inside the tent. Luther became fearful that something was wrong, and he ran and hid behind some trees. A short time later the strangers reappeared carrying bundles, then rode away.

The boy crept down to the tent and peered inside. A scene of horror greeted his eyes. The three occupants had been shot and mutilated with a meat cleaver.

According to the *Enterprise,* "Luther raced home, arriving about eight o'clock in the evening, very much excited. He made signs to his mother by beating himself with a stick, drawing his hand across his throat and pointing at his head as though leveling a pistol."

For once Mrs. Carey could not make out his meaning. But she understood it well on the following day when the bodies of the victims were discovered.

Afterward, the newspaper announced the deaths of the three men on the front page, claiming that "they were most brutally and outrageously murdered for plunder." It was also reported that young Luther had been able to identify three of the assailants, who were local residents.

At the second trial the defense summoned witnesses who claimed that both Duran and Lora had been elsewhere at the hour of the slayings. However, the alibis seemed to conflict, for one witness said they had been at home while another said he had seen them drinking in a saloon.

The entire case hinged on the testimony of Luther Carey, since he was the only eyewitness. The defense attorney asked the court to disqualify him as incompetent. Indeed, there was some doubt as to whether the sign interpreter had properly understood all the questions and whether he had managed to convey them properly to the boy and then grasp his answers.

Nevertheless, the judge overruled the attorney's request. In his opinion it was up to the jury to decide whether Luther's testimony was to be believed. Said the *Enterprise*, "The boy's words seemed to convince every disinterested person who heard it." They also convinced the jury.

"The jurymen were out about eight hours," said the paper, "and when they came in it was noticeable from their faces that they had performed a solemn and unpleasant duty. When the verdict of 'guilty of murder in the first degree' was announced, a tremor ran through the large crowd in the courthouse. If the prisoners were affected by the verdict, there was no visible sign."

As to the final outcome of the case, no information has thus far come to light, at least from the pages of the Silver City Enterprise. A good guess would be that the convicted parties met the appointment with their maker at the end of a hangman's rope.

New Mexico's Great Train Robbery

Mention train robberies in the Old West and one immediately thinks of Jesse James and the Dalton gang in Missouri and Kansas. But New Mexico had its share of train hold-ups too, though most have been forgotten.

The most sensational case in southwestern New Mexico occurred in late November 1883. The Southern Pacific was chugging along fifteen miles west of Deming when the fireman suddenly noticed that one of the rails had been torn out. He shouted to the engineer, a man named Webster, to put on the air brakes. Scarcely had the train ground to a halt when a hail of bullets from the brush struck the cab, killing the engineer instantly.

Five masked bandits then climbed aboard, emptied the express car, and robbed the passengers. In a few short minutes they were racing away on horseback with their loot. A brakeman hiked to the next station at Gage where word of the crime was flashed back to Deming. A posse was soon on the trail, but the culprits had vanished.

The incident caused excitement throughout the territory, and a reward of $17,500 was quickly posted for capture of the assailants. It was suspected that they were local men, and the investigation focused on the Silver City area. A search of nearby hills turned up a deserted camp believed to have been used by the robbers before the hold-up. At the dead campfire sheriff's deputies discovered an empty tin can that once held pickled pigs' feet.

A Southern Pacific train, shown here at El Paso del Norte
[Ciudad Juárez], June 1881. Photo by George C. Bennett.
Courtesy Museum of New Mexico. Neg. No. 14915.

Checking with grocers in Silver City, it was learned that two young men, Mitch Lee and Kit Joy, had recently purchased pigs' feet. That clue identified them as members of the gang and the search was on.

The outlaws were from prominent ranch families in southern New Mexico, and the oldest, Mitch Lee, was only twenty-four. None had been involved in trouble before, and many people could not believe they were guilty.

Lest anyone show them sympathy, the *Silver City Enterprise* warned readers: "Hunt them down, ranchmen and cowboys. They are your enemies, the enemies of law and order, and deprived an honest, hard-working engineer of his life, leaving his wife and children in destitute circumstances. Do not protect such villains by informing them of the movements of the officers."

The first of the gang to be apprehended was Frank Taggart. He was described as twenty-two years of age, five feet eight inches tall, 150 pounds, and having light hair and mustache, blue eyes, and a large mouth "which is always wreathed in smiles." That's scarcely the portrait of a hardened criminal.

One by one the other train robbers were captured and lodged in the Silver City jail to stand trial. Weeks passed and then on March 14, 1884, a startling headline appeared in the morning papers. "A BREAK FOR LIBERTY!" it read. The outlaws had escaped.

The circumstances were these. Each day the prisoners had been allowed out of their cells for exercise. But on this occasion they had managed to overpower the guards and lock them in the cell.

Young Mitch Lee brought a bucket of water from the well and placed it by the cell door, remarking that the guards would probably get thirsty before help came.

The gang, now heavily armed, had hurried to the Elephant Corral close by and stolen horses. When the alarm was sounded, the sheriff deputized every available man and gave chase.

Two miles outside Silver City the posse overtook the escapees and a furious gun battle ensued. It was as noisy and bloody a fight as ever pictured on the Hollywood screen.

Two of the robbers were killed and two others, Frank Taggart and Mitch Lee, were recaptured. Only Kit Joy managed to escape down a canyon.

On the way back to town with their prisoners, the posse decided to hold a necktie party. A U.S. marshal who was along ordered that the men be turned over to him. But the surly crowd told him to ride down to Fort Bayard and get a troop of cavalry to enforce his demand. Sheriff F. C. Cantley also protested against the hanging, saying he would never permit it while armed. The posse immediately relieved him of his arms.

As nooses were fitted over the necks of the condemned men, they were asked for any last words. Frank Taggart, he with the smiling face, complained of not getting a square deal. True, he had robbed the train, but it had been Lee who murdered Engineer Webster against the wishes of his companions.

Mitch Lee's final words were, "Well, by God! I did kill him." Jerked skyward, he died almost instantly. Not so his sandy-haired accomplice. According to a news reporter on the scene, "Taggart died hard of strangulation—a throat disease that is becoming extremely common among their ilk in this section."

A few weeks later, the remaining train robber, Kit Joy, was cornered and after exchanging gunfire with lawmen was captured. He had been severely wounded in the leg, however, and after being returned to Silver City, the limb had to be amputated below the knee.

It was not certain that he could get a fair trial in Grant County, so he was transferred to Hillsboro to await the next session of court there. It was generally agreed that "he would die upon the gallows." A friend at the time related that "Kit Joy is losing hope and doubtless feels that a restless and wicked life will soon close in a manner not pleasant to remember and disgraceful in its character."

The youth's disgrace was compounded by the fact that his parents owned a ranch in Hillsboro and boyhood friends were in attendance at his trial. The prosecutor was unable to prove that Joy had killed the engineer or even tried to do so. As a result, the jury brought in a verdict of guilty on a charge of second-degree murder. The young man was given a life sentence.

The trial brought to a close the story of the Southern Pacific train robbery. But what no one could ever explain was why a group of upstanding, courageous, and friendly young men should desert the honest path for a single, bloodstained escapade in crime.

A Desperate Gang of Thieves

"**T**hey are as desperate and villainous a gang of thieves as ever infested any country." That's how the outspoken *Silver City Enterprise* described the notorious Hall Gang, which began terrorizing southwestern New Mexico in 1887.

The evil Halls included "the old man" and his four strapping sons, all said to have served time in the Texas Penitentiary before landing in the New Mexico Territory. They first appeared at John Brockman's ranch on the Mimbres River in Grant County.

One day they drove some cattle onto his land and moved themselves into a vacant house. When Brockman protested, he was made to understand that he was dealing with a hard crowd and better hold his tongue.

Senseless cruelty was the Halls' stock-in-trade. Once they met a Chinese on the road who had been sent by his employer to pick up the mail. For no reason, they pistol-whipped the poor fellow nearly to death.

The main activity of the family was rustling cattle. In that shady business they were well experienced. Ranchers throughout western New Mexico began to suffer wholesale losses. So extensive did these operations become that the Halls found it necessary to bring in large numbers of accomplices, all as tough and mean as themselves.

The gang was as brutal to animals as it was to people. Cows with new calves were stolen and driven to a secluded place in the mountains. There the mothers were roped and killed, the outlaws beating them over the head with rocks. The orphaned calves were then herded to the Hall ranch and marked with their brand.

Stolen mares with suckling colts got the same treatment. Apparently killing the mothers was part of the Halls' scheme for concealing their crimes. They would skin the animals and burn the hides to destroy the brands.

Within a couple of years, the gang's original herd of 200 cattle had increased to 2,000 head. And in one season, their two brood mares appeared to produce nine two-year-old colts, "a most remarkable increase," neighbors bitterly noted.

And the outlaws had another trick to acquire stock. They would ride about putting the owners' own brand on new calves, but branding lightly so as to merely scorch the hair. When the ranch cowboys checked the herds for unbranded calves, they bypassed those with the scorch marks. Later, when the animals had grown large enough to be driven long distances, the Halls would return, carry them off, and after burning their own permanent brand, make a "legal" sale.

That the gang went so long unchallenged, almost four years, can be laid to its power and threats of violence. Prominent ranchers between Silver City and the Arizona line lived under constant fear of assassination. The slim resources of the law seemed inadequate to deal with the situation.

Finally, Thomas Lyons, superintendent of the huge L. C. Cattle Company, decided something had to be done. That was after the Hall brothers bragged loudly that they had killed thirty L. C. mother cows and left the carcasses in a pit.

"The Day Herd," cowboys and cattle in New Mexico. Courtesy Museum of New Mexico. Neg. No. 104688.

Said the *Enterprise* in a ringing editorial: "The situation is certainly very grave and will doubtless end in bloodshed. The time has now come to draw the line. These thieves and outlaws must be put down for once and for ever. Men who believe in maintaining law and order should come to the front and show their hand."

Worried that such a thing might actually happen, the Halls and a dozen cutthroats rode up to the L. C. ranch house, planning to gun down Mr. Lyons. One man with backbone, they knew, could set the whole country against them.

Luckily Lyons was not at home and the murdering band departed in angry silence. But when word of their intent spread, so did the opposition. Deputy

Sheriff John Johnson now obtained warrants of arrest and began to form a posse. Some men, out of fear, refused to join. But enough others answered the call to provide the deputy with a formidable army.

Several of the culprits were arrested, but the main part of the band, it was learned, had camped at the Bates ranch in Bear Valley. One of the Hall women, captured earlier, broke away from the posse and rode like a demon to give the alarm. A rancher said afterward, "The devil couldn't have stopped her!"

The woman galloped up to the hideout shouting, "A mob! A mob! They're killing everyone in this valley." The outlaws scattered like a flock of chickens just as the posse arrived. There followed a rough-and-tumble chase on horseback, in the best tradition of a Hollywood B western.

The prisoners were brought to Silver City and safely lodged in the county jail, "a thing which could not have been accomplished in any other western settlement," declared the local press.

And it added, "These outlaws had stolen, burned, buffaloed, bulldozed, and harassed the settlers for over three years. The only wonder is that the prisoners ever reached the jail alive. While such measures are to be deplored, yet who would censure the victims had they exterminated such a horde."

The paper, in effect, seemed to be condoning vigilante justice. But it had to settle for the fact that enough evidence existed to insure each of the accused a long prison term. And thus ended, in 1891, the Hall family's vicious reign of terror.

The Apache Kid's Last Raid

In the 1880s and 1890s a renegade Indian known as the Apache Kid committed a series of brutal crimes in southern New Mexico and Arizona. Traveling alone or with one or two companions, he seems to have preyed as much on his own people as upon white men. The exact number of persons he caught in some isolated area and killed will never be known.

About the mid-90s the Kid dropped from sight, and it was supposed at the time that he had slipped into northern Mexico looking for safety in the Sierra Madres. Historians have remained uncertain of his fate. But a story related some time ago by an old-timer provides one explanation of how the Apache Kid met his end.

In 1907 a man named Billy Keene was living in the small mining camp of Chloride at the foot of the Black Range northwest of present Truth or Consequences. Among other occupations, he served as a guide during hunting season. At this time he was preparing to take into the mountains a party from the Swift Packing Company of Chicago.

Before he could hit the trail, however, word reached Chloride that horse thieves had run off animals belonging to residents north of town. Six men formed a posse to give chase, and Billy Keene was elected leader.

The men rode north stopping at ranches every now and then and asking whether anyone looking suspicious had gone by. At the ranch of Sebe Sorrels, they learned of fresh tracks belonging to the thieves

Chloride, New Mexico, ca. 1890-95. Photo by
Henry A. Schmidt. Courtesy Museum of New Mexico.
Neg. No. 13782.

which pointed toward the distant San Mateo Mountains. The posse put spurs to its horses and raced on.

As dark settled in, Keene spotted a campfire far
up on the San Mateo divide. Evidently the culprits,
whoever they were, had no inkling of pursuit and
had gotten careless.

The pursuers traveled all night, and by dawn's
first glimmer they were hidden in the pines above a
sloping meadow where the lost horses were grazing.
Keene saw a wisp of smoke from below and knew it

was the fire of the thieves. He signaled his men to remain concealed and quiet.

Shortly two Indians came striding up the slope toward the animals. The one in the lead was large and powerful with a sinister look about him. Cradled in one arm was a Winchester. The second figure was much smaller and trailed some thirty yards behind.

Billy Keene quickly decided that if they tried to capture the pair there would surely be a fight and a few of his own companions might be hurt. So he gave a sign to the two men next to him and they fired in unison. Struck by three bullets, the larger Indian was knocked over backward, and his rifle flew into the air.

At once the one behind dashed into the timber with lead swarming around him and disappeared. When Billy went over to the edge of the trees, he found a lot of blood. So he believed that the second Indian had received a mortal wound.

The posse regrouped and walked down to the smoldering campfire. There they discovered evidence that a woman with two babies had fled at the first sound of gunfire. It was all very strange, since no renegade Indians had been seen in this area for many years.

The men went through the camp equipment and took what they wanted, including several silver bracelets. Everything else they threw on the fire and burned before heading back to Chloride with the horses. The body of the horse thief was left where it fell.

Later that same day, cowboy Ralph Turner rode into his line shack on the north side of the San

Mateos, some forty miles from where the shooting had occurred. He was startled to see a much-bedraggled Indian woman dodge out of his cabin. She had helped herself to food scraps from his table.

Getting several neighbors to accompany him, Turner followed the woman's footprints a short distance to a pinyon tree. Here they observed signs that two babies in cradle boards had been left briefly tied to one of the limbs. The woman had placed them there while she went scavenging for food.

The cowboys followed the trail a bit longer, but when it left the mountains and headed east toward the Rio Grande, they gave up and returned home.

Much later that night, the fugitive with her youngsters was arrested at San Marcial, a railroad town downriver from Socorro. She had been going through the garbage cans behind the Harvey House restaurant when the sheriff caught her.

When questioned in Spanish, she claimed to be the wife of the notorious Apache Kid. White men had killed her husband in the San Mateo Mountains, and she was running from them with her children. She said she was glad the Kid was dead since he had often beaten her and kept her chained in camp. Whenever he wanted another woman, he would raid the reservation, steal a young girl, then kill her when he was tired of her.

Word carried to Chloride, and Billy Keene was much astonished to learn that he had slain a famous outlaw. His hunting clients from the Swift Packing Company arrived shortly afterward, and upon hearing the story, they asked Billy to ride back to the San Mateos and bring in the head of the Apache Kid.

He did, carting it home in a gunnysack tied to

his saddlehorn. In his front yard, a block from the Chloride post office, he set an iron kettle of water to boiling and threw in the head. When the grisly trophy was reduced to a bleached skull, he presented it to the company men. They went back to Chicago proudly bearing their souvenir of the wild and wicked West.

The Southwest's Great Impostor

On a brisk morning in 1897, a slender, white-haired man accompanied by a U.S. deputy marshal stepped from a carriage at the New Mexico penitentiary and walked up the steps to the superintendent's office. Thirty minutes later, he emerged with shaven head and clad in prison garb. James Addison Reavis, who for a quarter century had claimed to be the Baron of Arizona and owner of a twelve-million-acre Spanish land grant, was now convict number 964.

Reavis's crafty fraud and his nearly successful attempt to establish claim over the bogus Peralta grant must be rated as one of the most fantastic episodes in southwestern history. It began in the 1870s in St. Louis where James Reavis was struggling to make a living selling real estate. By chance he made the acquaintance of a certain George M. Willing, who had purchased some papers dated 1758, alleged to be a land grant from the King of Spain to Don Miguel Nemecio Silva de Peralta. The grant comprised a tract of 50 by 150 square miles in southern Arizona and New Mexico, extending from Phoenix east to the vicinity of Silver City.

At Willing's request, Reavis agreed to assist in investigating the title and having it confirmed by the U. S. government. The two men went to Prescott, Arizona Territory, about 1875, and there Willing died under mysterious circumstances, apparently the victim of poison. That left Reavis in possession of the grant papers.

Over the next several years, he worked upon the case and in 1883 filed a petition with the surveyor general of Arizona, asking that his claim to the Peralta grant be recognized. His move threw thousands of people living in the area into a panic. Among them were farmers who had established homesteads and persons with mining claims. Many of them hurried to make terms with Reavis by paying him for quit claim deeds.

Large companies also joined the stampede to Reavis's door. The Southern Pacific Railroad paid him $50,000 for right of way through his alleged grant. And the Silver King Mining Company gave him $25,000 for a release of his claim on their mines. In this way he quickly piled up an immense fortune. Some of the biggest names in American business, on both the East and West coasts, were soon numbered among his friends, and they joined in urging that the government confirm his grant.

From the start James Reavis knew that his Spanish documents, on close examination, might not hold up in court; so once he had accumulated a healthy bank account he set about to strengthen his case. As a start he presented to public view his new wife, Dona Sofia Loreta Micaela de Peralta, a native

111

of California and supposedly the great-granddaughter and only living heir of the original grantee. According to his story, he had met her by chance on a train near Sacramento.

Next Reavis visited archives in Spain and Mexico and turned up documents seeming to show the early history of the Peralta family in the Southwest. They revealed that Don Miguel Nemecio Peralta had been a nobleman sent to New Spain (Mexico) by Philip V to investigate certain governmental affairs. He had performed his duties so well that the grateful king bestowed upon him the title of Baron of Arizona and granted him the huge piece of real estate now claimed by Reavis.

Upon his death Peralta had willed both his title and lands to his only son, and through him they had passed to Reavis's wife, the only surviving member of the family. Upon this evidence, James Reavis now claimed for himself the title, Baron of Arizona. If he could win confirmation of the lands too, he would be the largest property owner in the United States. And he came within a whisper of taking the grand prize.

In 1893 he asked the Court of Private Land Claims at Santa Fe to confirm the grant. In support he presented an impressive array of documents accumulated on his trips to the archives: royal decrees, wills, deeds, birth certificates of members of the Peralta family, and so on. Four outstanding lawyers surveyed the material and pronounced it genuine. In addition, a host of witnesses were produced who claimed to have known Mrs. Reavis since her birth and who could testify that she was the legal Peralta heir.

New Mexico penitentiary photo by James Addison Reavis
(No. 964). Courtesy Museum of New Mexico. Neg. No. 50327.

But one man was still not convinced. He was Matthew Reynolds, attorney for the Court of Land Claims, who had been designated by the government to challenge Reavis's papers. From Santa Fe, he sent investigators to Spain, Mexico, and California, and what they discovered broke the case open. In Spain Reavis had been caught tampering with the archives at Seville and had been forced to flee the country, a fugitive.

At the Mexican archive in Guadalajara, Reynolds's investigator found that original documents had been removed from the record and forgeries, pertaining to the Barony of Arizona, substituted in their place. In California it was learned that Reavis had spent $50,000 purchasing witnesses who would authenticate the tale of his wife's noble descent. She was in fact not a Peralta at all, and Don Miguel Nemecio Peralta had never existed.

All Reavis's claims were rejected. He was arrested on charges of conspiring to defraud the United States, was tried, convicted, and imprisoned. The Department of Justice in its annual report for 1895 referred to the Reavis swindle in this way: "The case is remarkable as probably the greatest fraud ever attempted against a government in its own courts."

Lawmen on Horseback

Everyone has heard of the Canadian Mounties—those daring men in red coats who sit erect in the saddle and fearlessly keep the peace. But who today recalls the New Mexico Mounties? Unfortunately, memory of that small but splendid band of lawmen has just about disappeared.

The New Mexico Mounted Police, known popularly as "the Mounties," existed for less than twenty years in the early part of this century. But in that brief time they compiled an enviable record of bravery and devotion to duty. They were also the forerunners of our modern State Police.

The New Mexico Territory in the first years of the twentieth century still had the look and the feel of the Old West about it. For one thing, it remained an outlaw haven. Texas Rangers on the east, Arizona Rangers on the west, and Mexican Rurales to the south had proven so effective in their cleanup operations that badmen found New Mexico the only safe hiding place.

Cattlemen, sheepmen, farmers, and even the railroads here began to lodge complaints with the government in Santa Fe. Rustlers and hold-up artists had become a plague on the territory.

In his message to the legislature in 1905, Governor Miguel Otero urged the passage of a "Ranger Law" which would provide men to patrol the ranges and aid in the arrest of criminals. Newspapers around the territory applauded his recommendation.

Senator W. H. Greer, a wealthy rancher from Bernalillo, took the lead in drafting a bill. He decided that the new lawmen should be called mounted policemen rather than rangers.

For one thing, New Mexico earlier had a group of unofficial rangers headed by an ex-gunslinger named Tom Tucker. Their checkered history had left

Fred Lambert and Emily Tefft, Cimarron, New Mexico,
April 23, 1968. When he died in 1971, Lambert was the last
of the New Mexico Mounted Police. Photo by Henry D. Tefft.
Courtesy Museum of New Mexico. Neg. No. 137713.

the name "ranger" somewhat tainted. Knowing of the prestige of the Royal Canadian Mounted Police, Senator Greer concluded that in borrowing their name he would also be borrowing some of their good reputation.

So, a Mounted Police Law was passed by the legislature, creating an initial force of eleven men. Captain John F. Fullerton became commander, with headquarters at Socorro near the center of the territory. Each mountie was outfitted with saddle and pack horses and with Winchester rifles and Colt six-guns.

At once a newspaper in Alamogordo praised the new mounted police, describing the men as, "experienced, all dead shots, who can be relied on to capture or kill." The paper suggested they begin their work in the Animas Mountains down in the far southwestern corner of the territory. There, it reported, were desperate outlaws, driven into the mountains by the Texas and Arizona Rangers and the Mexican Rurales.

In fact, that was precisely where the Mounties launched their operations. Lieutenant Capriano Baca, second in command, led his fellow lawmen in a raid that purged that section of the territory of criminals. It proved a good beginning.

Sometimes the Mounties worked as a group, but individual chases, of the kind made famous by the Texas Rangers, were not uncommon. Sergeant Bob Lewis, on the trail of a desperado, disappeared for several months. His family had no idea where he was. When the sergeant finally reappeared with his man in custody, he learned that in the interim his small daughter had died. His dedication to duty became an example for other Mounties.

Only one incident marred the short history of the Mounted Police. A paper, the *Albuquerque Daily Citizen,* published a slanted story in 1907 about Lieutenant Baca which forced his resignation from the force. It claimed he had gotten drunk and destroyed a telephone in a saloon fight at the village of San Antonio, near Socorro.

In an interview with the rival *Albuquerque Journal*, Baca defended his actions. "I'm sorry," he declared, "that the *Daily Citizen* thinks I'm cruel enough to smash an innocent and defenseless telephone. Anyway, the telephone is smashed although I did not do it.

"The facts are few and brief. Myself, with several other friends were in the saloon mentioned in San Antonio. So was the telephone. It was unfortunate for the telephone, but we could not prevent its presence. At any rate, we had a drink or so and presently several of the boys engaged in a friendly scuffle, in which somebody got shoved against the wall and the unfortunate telephone.

"The telephone got knocked from its fastenings and smashed. That is all there is to it. I do not think, however, that I should have been convicted of assaulting the telephone without a hearing."

Even though the numerous witnesses claimed Baca was innocent, the episode gave the Mounties bad publicity and he resigned. The force lost one of its best men.

Over the years ordinary citizens were pleased with the performance of the Mounties. But not so, many politicians. Corruption has always been a part of New Mexico government, at all levels, and wrongdoers in high places feared the broad powers of the Mounted Police. From the beginning there were constant efforts to abolish the force.

Those efforts succeeded on February 15, 1921, when the state legislature passed "An Act to Repeal the Law Relating to the New Mexico Mounted Police." The mounties were no more! Another fifteen years would pass before the present State Police Force was created.

The Last Train Robbery

Train robberies were supposed to have gone out of style after the James and Dalton gangs were broken up and Black Jack Ketchum was hanged. But two young men from the East apparently did not get the message. In 1938 they bungled their way through an episode of banditry that was fifty years or more behind the times.

The leader, Henry Lorenz, was twenty-two and the younger of the luckless pair. He had been born in Germany in a detention camp during World War I. Later his family immigrated to New York, where Henry became addicted to western magazines and western movies. He badgered his father constantly to buy him high-heeled boots and a big hat.

Mr. Lorenz, however, did not believe in such foolishness. Not only did he refuse to buy boots and a hat for his son, he took away his magazines. That was too much for Henry.

He ran away from home and got a job in a shoe store. In time, he saved five hundred dollars. He also befriended another foreign-born youth, a curly-

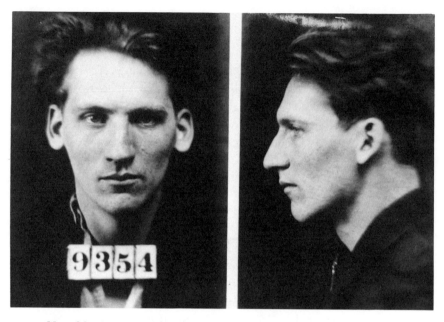

New Mexico penitentiary photo of Henry Lorenz (No. 9354), 1938. Courtesy New Mexico State Records Center and Archives, Santa Fe.

haired Frenchman named Harry Dwyer.

"Come along, Harry, I'll stake you to a trip," Henry said. We'll go west and be cowboys." It all sounded quite romantic, far better than sweating one's life away clerking in a store.

The boys landed in El Paso and took a room in a cheap hotel. Then they promptly went out and bought cowboy boots and hats plus horses and saddles. They made several trips between El Paso and Deming, and on one of these they brought back two girls. With all this gadding about, their money went

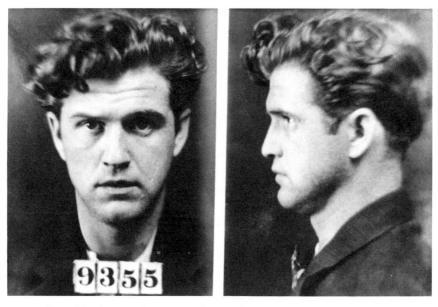

New Mexico penitentiary photo of Harry Dwyer (No. 9355), 1938, Courtesy New Mexico State Records Center and Archives, Santa Fe.

fast, especially after they acquired their lady friends.

The horses and saddles had to be sold, but even so, the boys were soon nearly broke. "We'll go farther west, to Arizona or California," declared Henry. "Maybe our luck will change out there."

Imagining what Billy the Kid might do, they decided to hold up a train to get enough money for their trip. With their last dollars, they bought tickets to Las Cruces on the westbound Southern Pacific, No. 11, known as "The Apache."

Along the way, Henry and Harry stood up in the day coach, pulled their pistols, and announced the hold-up. Marching the conductor up the aisle, Henry collected money and jewelry from the right side of the car. His companion followed some distance behind working the left.

At the rear, Henry ordered the conductor to stop the train and he prepared to get off. But looking back he saw that Harry was in serious trouble. Someone had tripped the novice bandit, and when he hit the floor a crowd of enraged passengers jumped on him.

Henry lost his head. One tall man stood above the others, and the boy shot and killed him in an instant. The victim was W. L. Smith, an employee of the railroad on his way to San Francisco. Henry fired again and struck another man. But fortunately the bullet glanced off a metal cigarette case in his breast pocket and fell harmlessly into his trouser cuff.

Momentarily stunned by this violent deed, Henry offered little resistance when other bystanders overpowered him. He was soon covered with bruises from a vicious pummeling. Poor Harry had one eye almost torn from its socket. In that hapless condition, they were shortly turned over to a posse.

The two modern-day desperados came to trial on February 19, 1938, at District Court in Las Cruces. On advice of their court-appointed attorney, they pleaded guilty to second-degree murder.

The shooting and subsequent trial created a sensation in the newspapers. The railroad demanded vengeance, and the widow of the slain Smith told the Las Cruces papers that she wanted "an eye for an eye." Eastern papers gave the case front-page coverage after they discovered that a couple of drugstore cowboys from New York had shot their way into the annals of western badmen.

In the courtroom, the "badmen" proved to be a couple of scared and contrite youths. "All I can say, sir, is I'm sorry," Henry told the judge. "I didn't mean to do it. I didn't plan to kill anyone. It was an accident."

And Harry added: "I'll spend all of my life making up for it, sir, if you'll go easy on us."

Public opinion, however, was running high, and the judge could hardly afford to be lenient. Smith had left not only a widow, but a small daughter suffering from tuberculosis. The circumstances argued for a stiff sentence. The boys were given fifty to seventy-five years in the State Penitentiary.

The tragic little drama had played itself out to a bitter end. Among the spectators leaving the scene of the trial one was overheard to remark, "Imagine those scoundrels thinking they could come here and pull that Wild West stuff on us!"

A useful starting point for any reading program on the subject is the 800-page book, *Six-Guns and Saddle Leather: A Bibliography of Books and Pamphlets on Western Outlaws and Gunmen* (Second revised edition; Norman: University of Oklahoma Press, 1969), which was compiled by the distinguished western author Ramon F. Adams. It lists nearly 2,500 works on law and lawlessness in the Old West and includes Adams's critical and often humorous annotations.

Among the older, general studies of outlaws, Eugene Cunningham's *Triggernometry: A Gallery of Gunfighters* (New York: Press of the Pioneers, 1934; and later editions) remains the best as far as readability and accuracy go, although his section on Billy the Kid is now outdated, having been superseded by more recent works. Controversies surrounding the Kid are dealt with most ably by Ramon F. Adams in his *A Fitting Death for Billy the Kid* (Norman: University of Oklahoma Press, 1960); while background on him is provided by John P. Wilson, *Merchants, Guns & Money: The Story of Lincoln County and Its Wars* (Santa Fe: Museum of New Mexico Press, 1987).

The following books dealing with specific outlaws can be recommended: on Clay Allison, Black Jack Ketchum, and other New Mexico desperados, see Agnes Morely Cleaveland's, *Satan's Paradise* (Boston: Houghton Mifflin, 1952); on Vicente Silva, a useful source is Tom McGrath, *Vicente Silva and His Forty Thieves* (Las Vegas, New Mexico: privately printed, 1960); on Ike Stockton, consult Eleanor D. McDonald and John Brown Arrington, *The San Juan Basin* (Denver: Green Mountain Press, 1970); and on the Apache Kid and Black Jack Ketchum, read Ben W. Kemp, *Cow Dust and Saddle Leather* (Norman: University of Oklahoma Press, 1968).

Books that give the lawman's side of the story include: Leon C. Metz, *Pat Garrett: The Story of a Western Lawman* (Norman: University of Oklahoma Press, 1973); Dee Harkey, *Mean As Hell* (Albuquerque: University of New Mexico Press, 1948; reprint, Ancient City Press, 1990); Charles A. Siringo, *The Cowboy Detective* (Lincoln: University of Nebraska Press, 1988); and Larry D. Ball, *The United States Marshals of New Mexico and Arizona* (Albuquerque: University of New Mexico Press, 1978).

Finally, note should be taken of a recent title that offers much on outlawry in old Las Vegas, New Mexico. It is Howard Bryan's *Wildest of the Wild West* (Santa Fe: Clear Light Publishers, 1988).